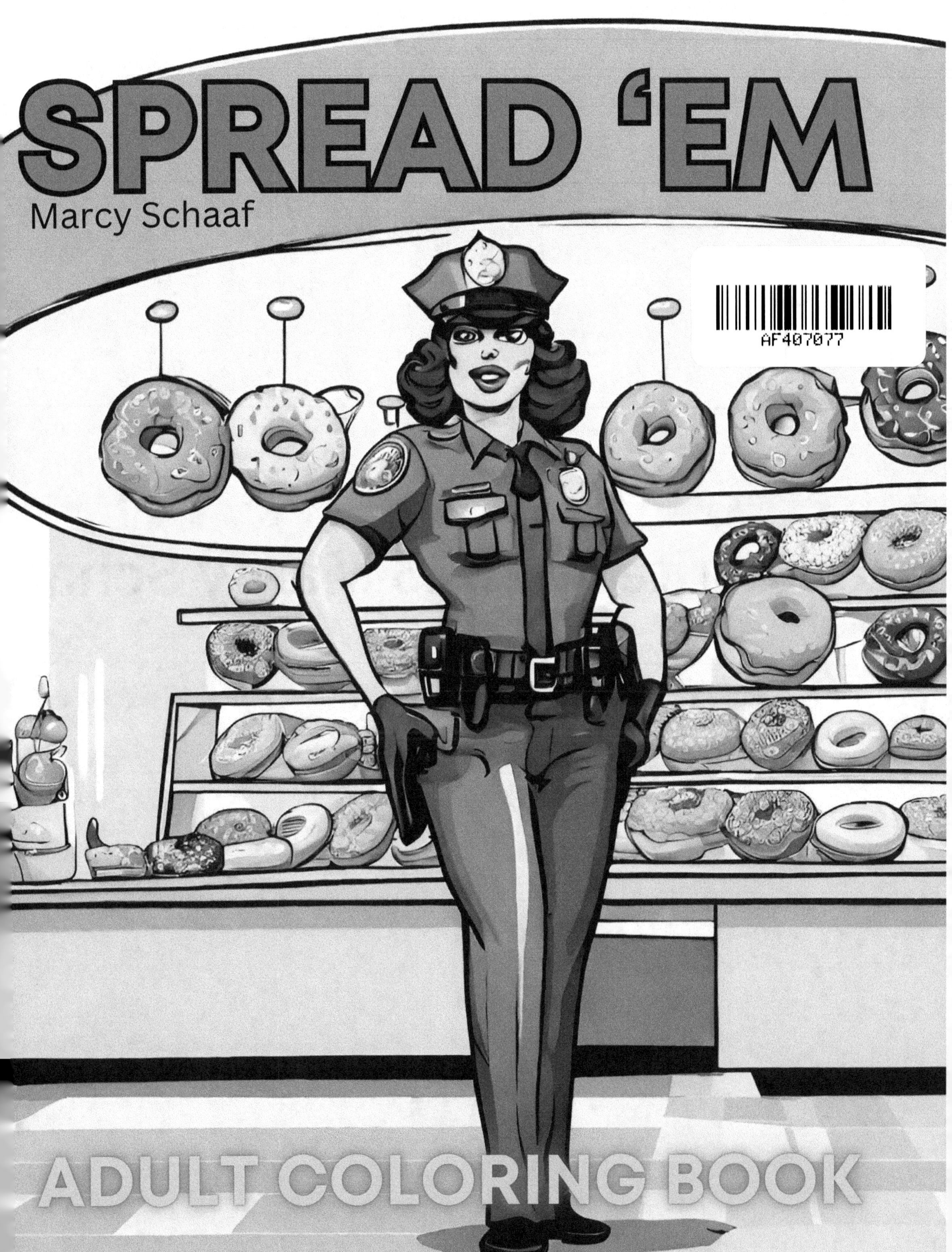

SPREAD 'EM
Marcy Schaaf
AF407077
ADULT COLORING BOOK

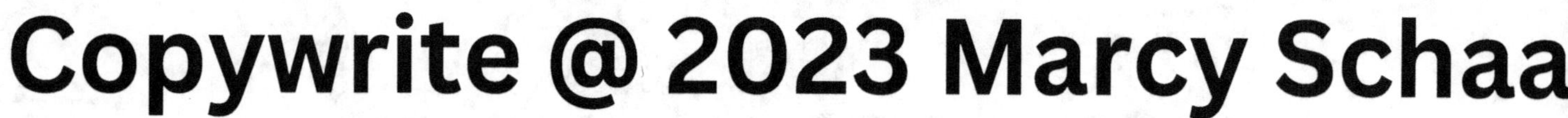

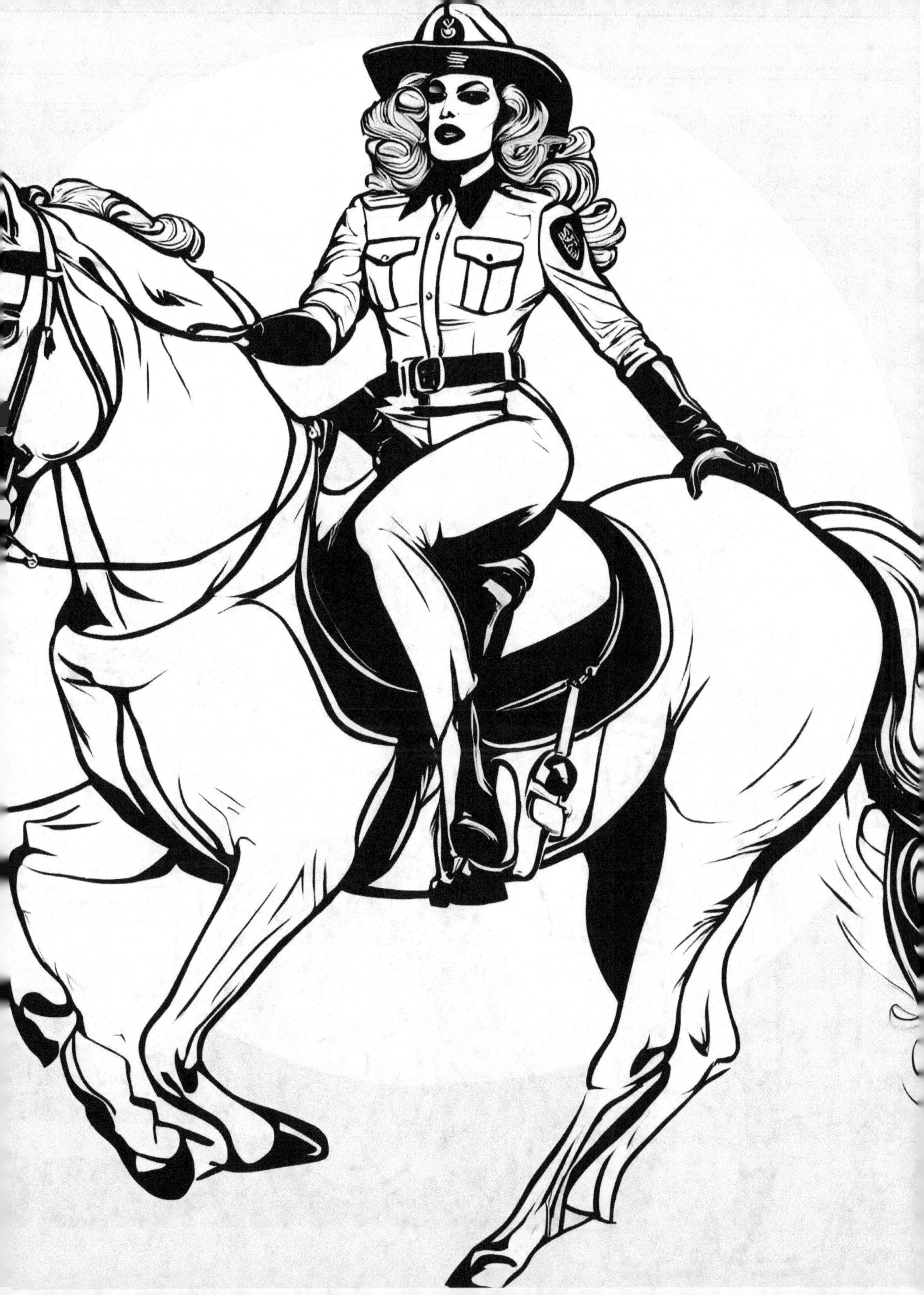

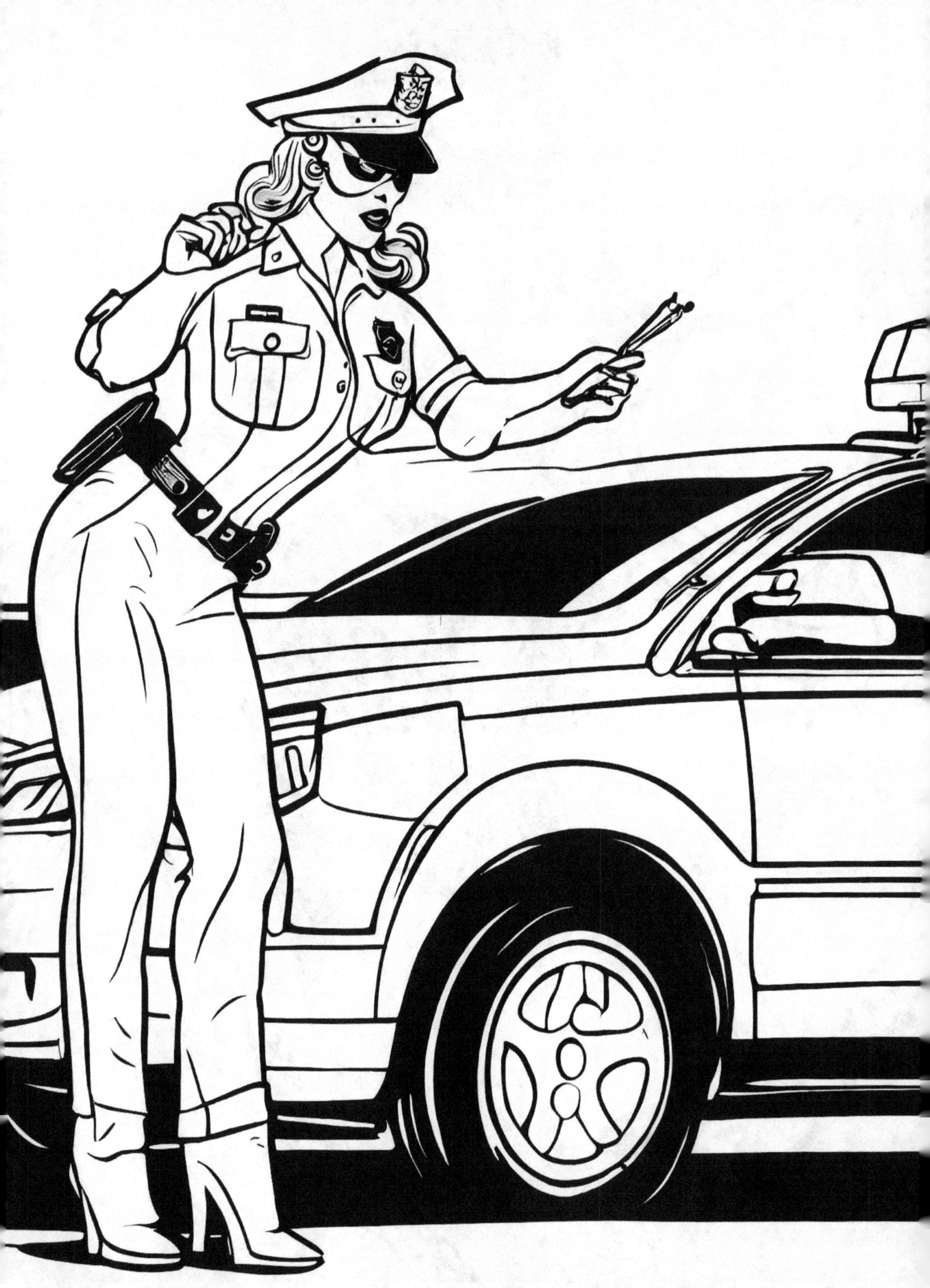

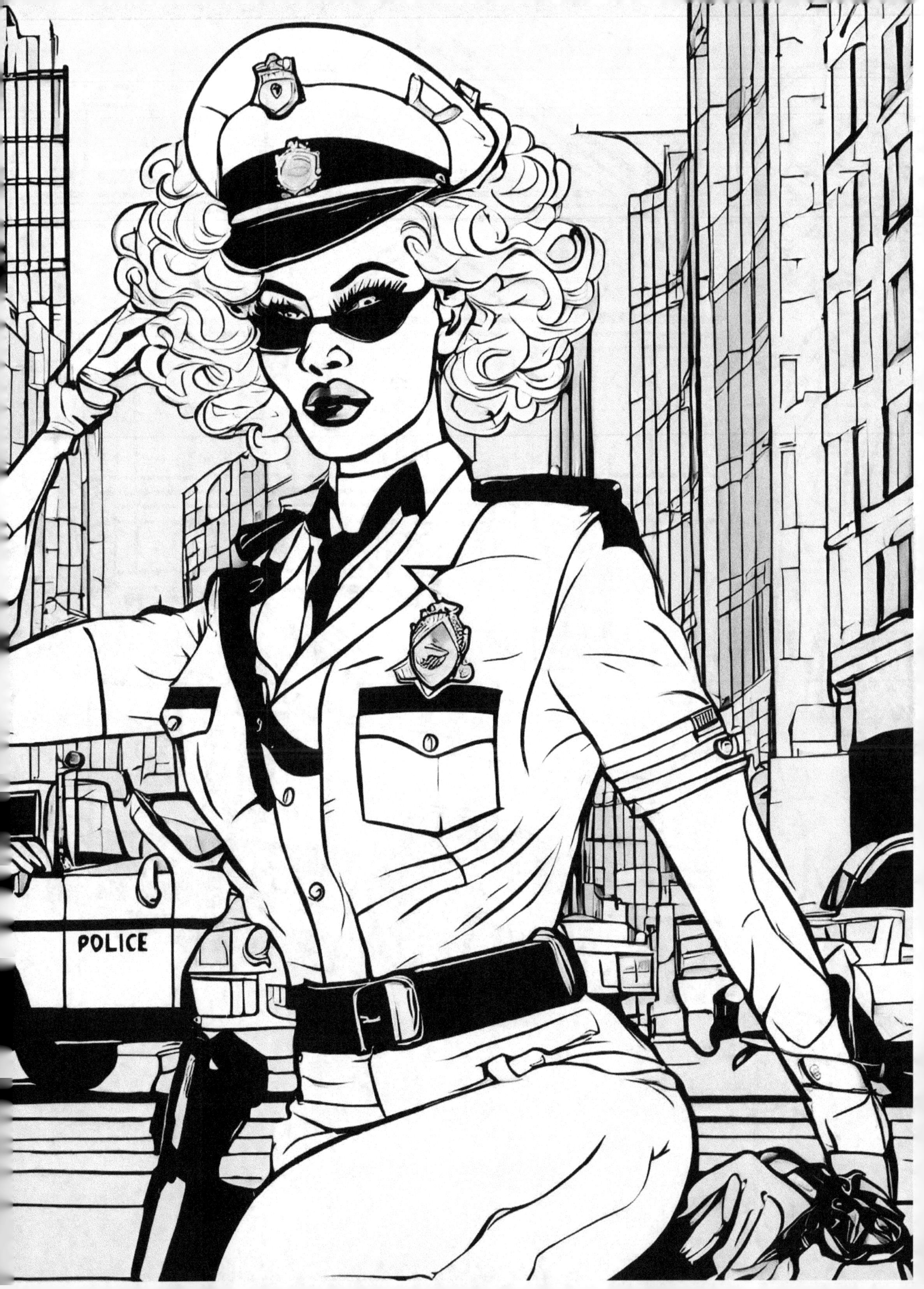
POLICE

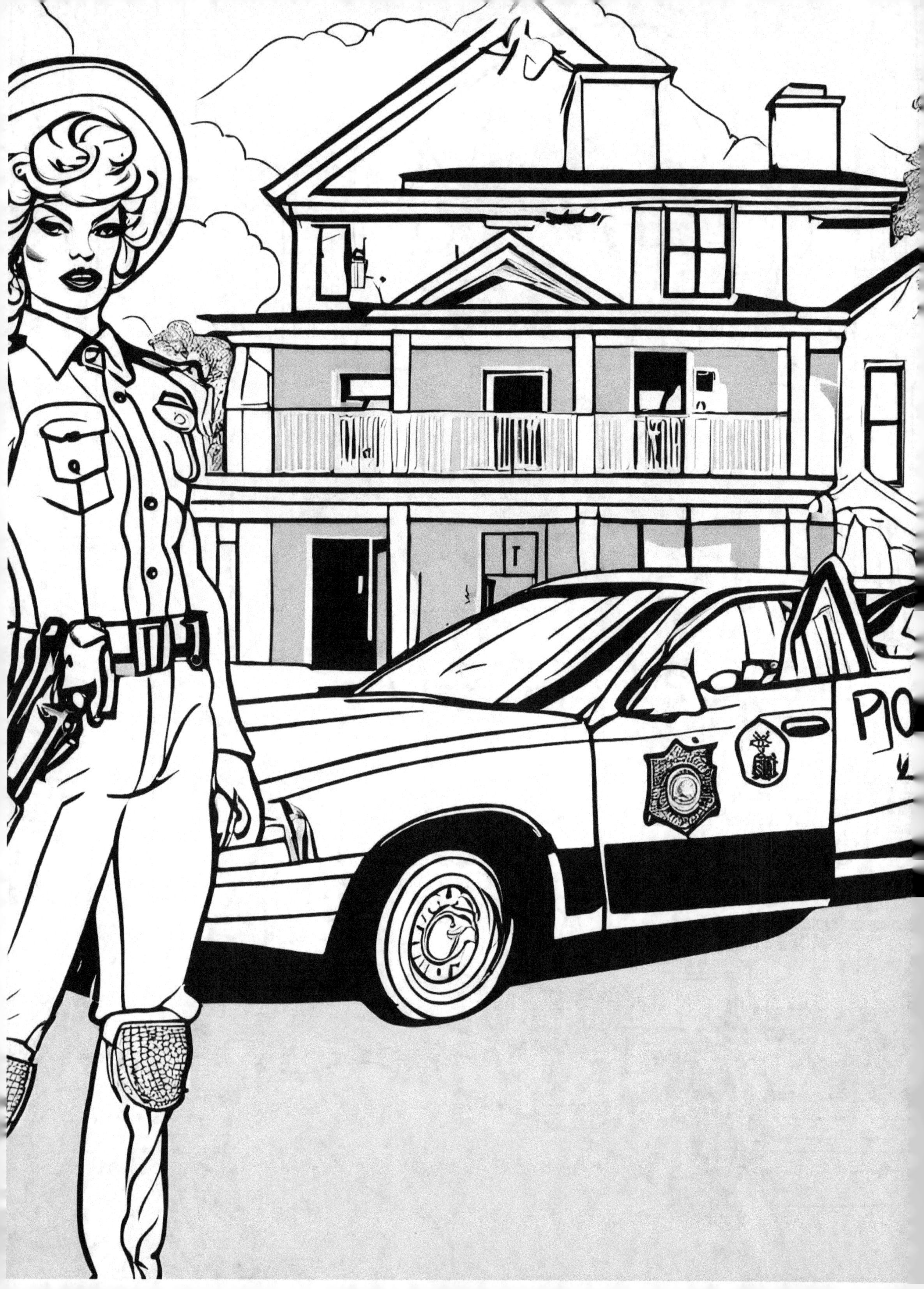
PO

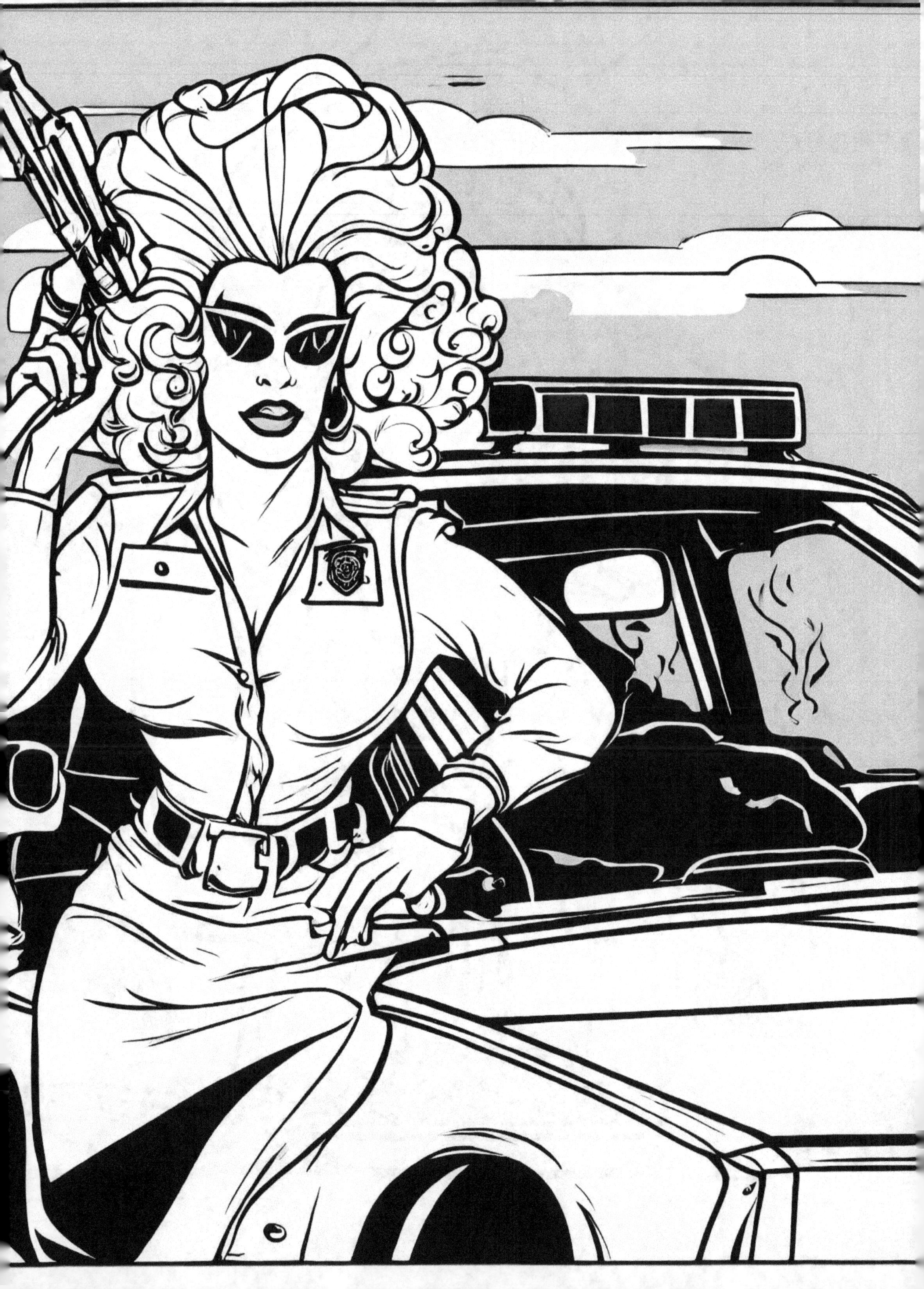

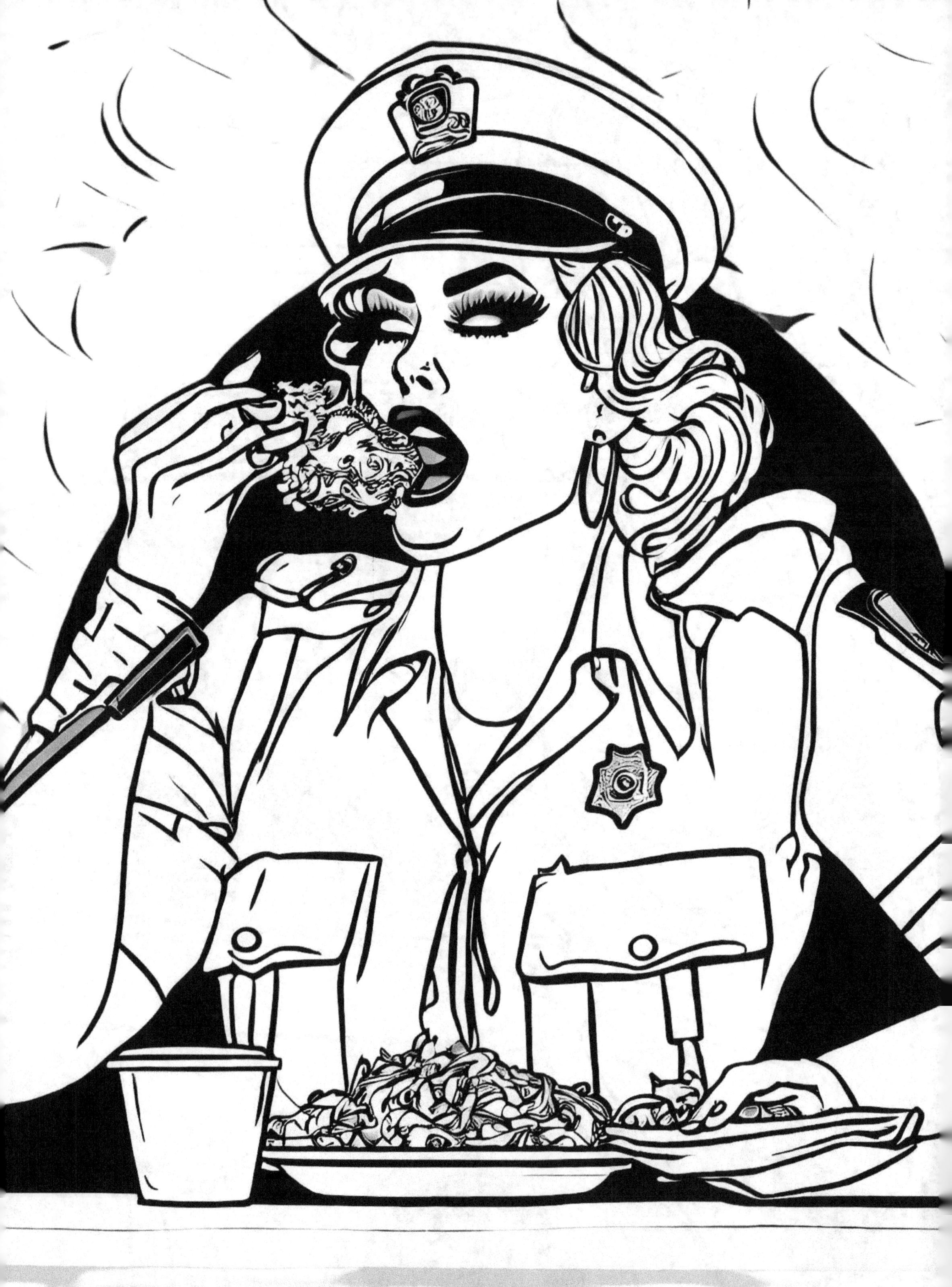

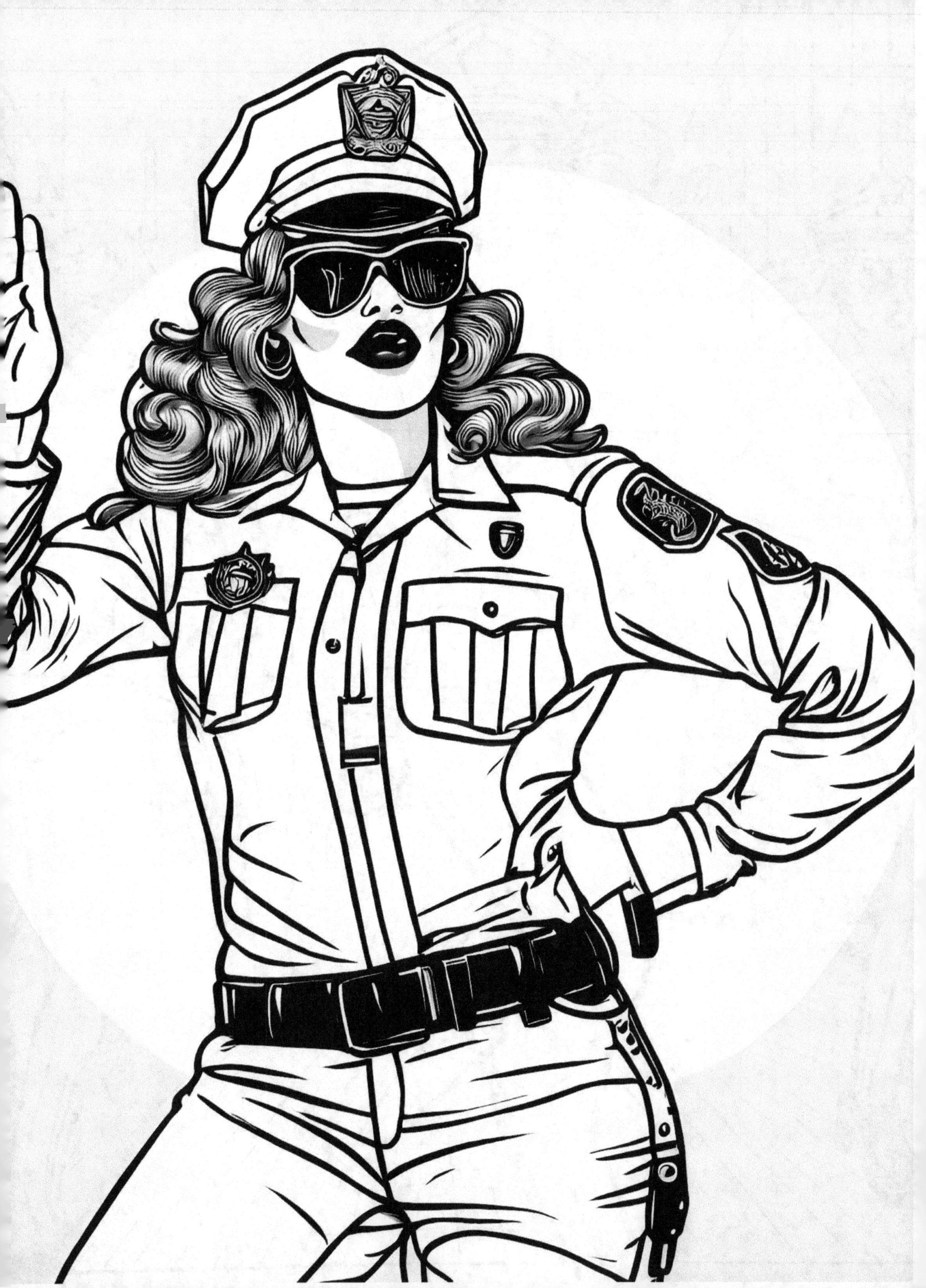

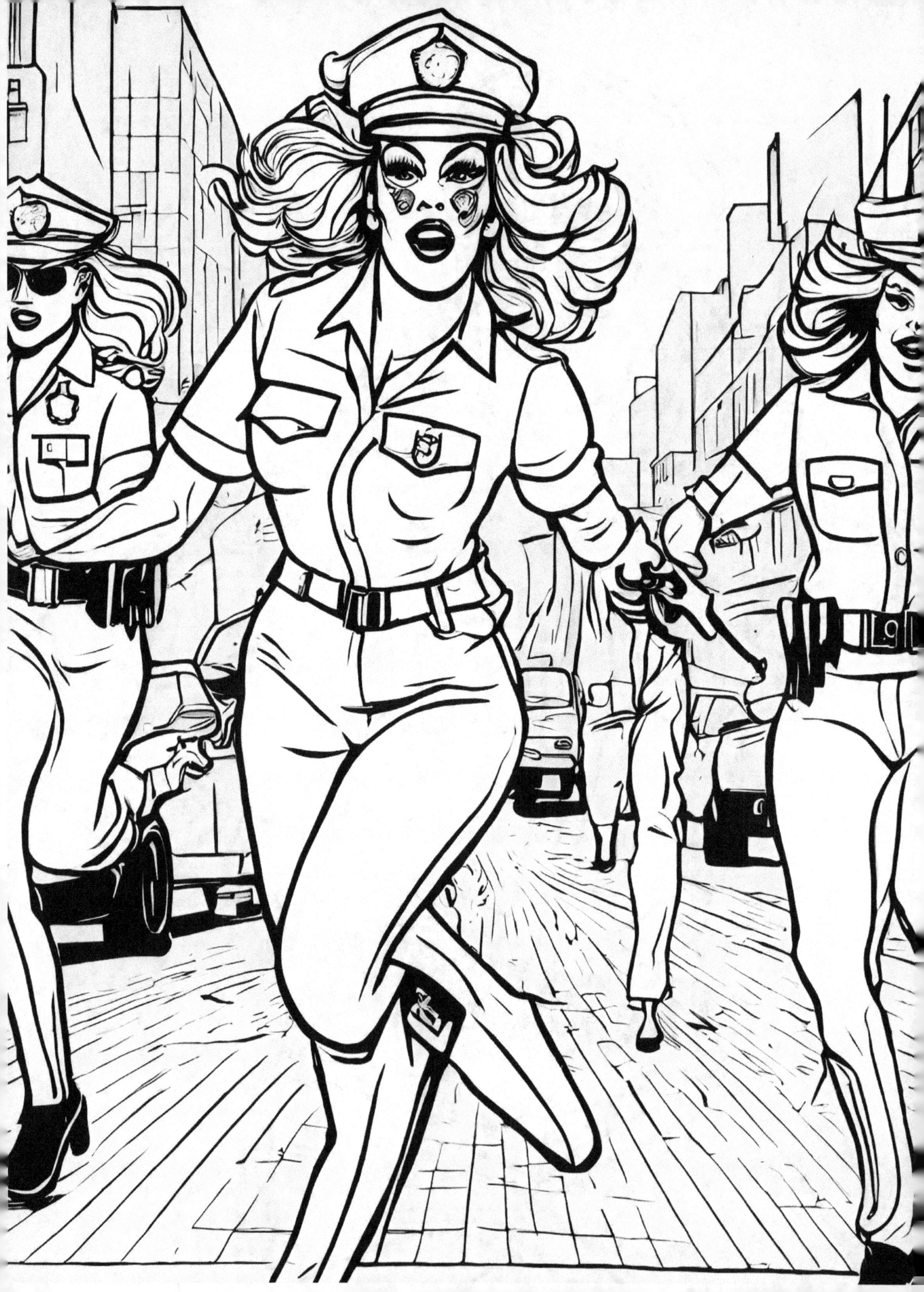

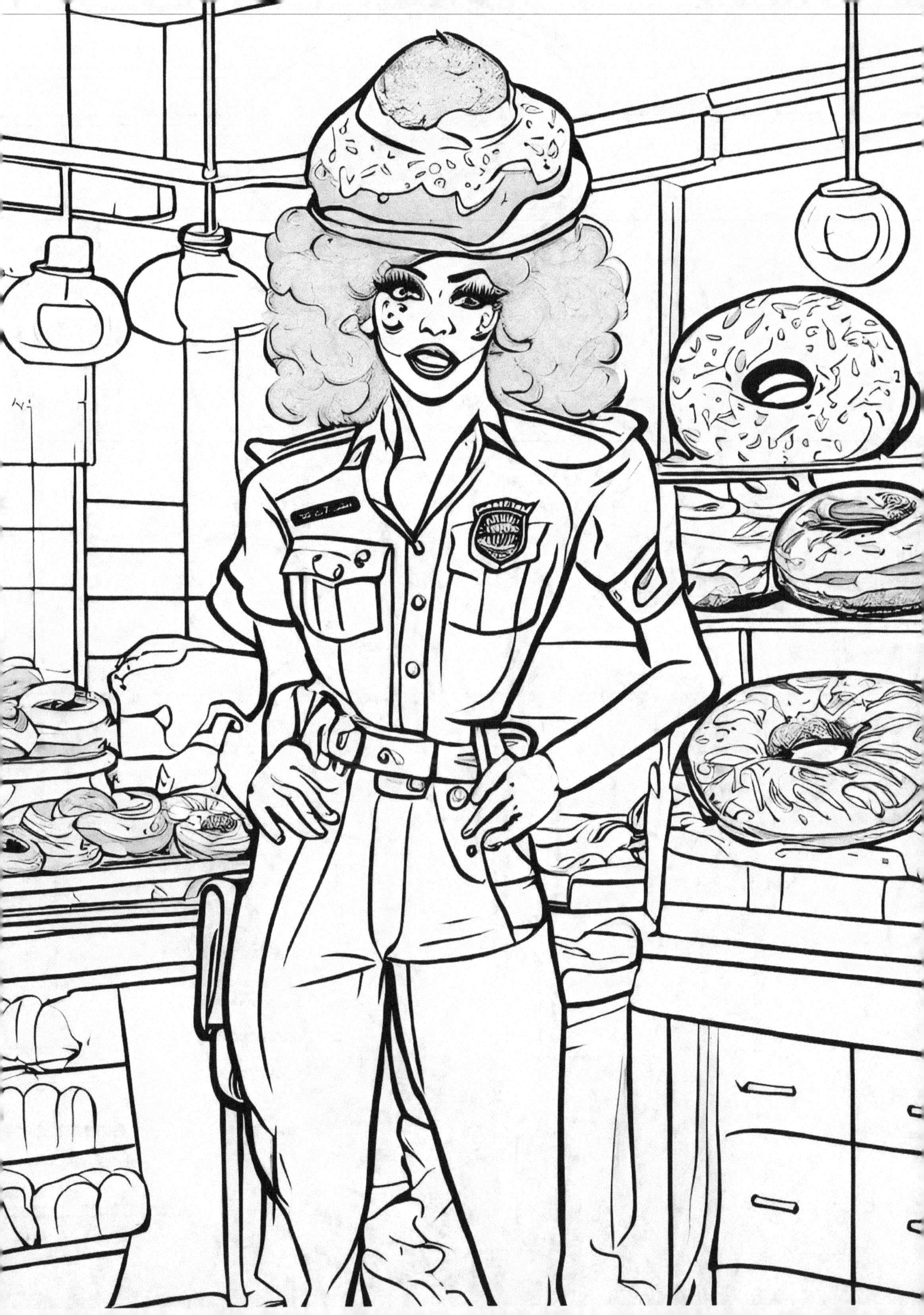

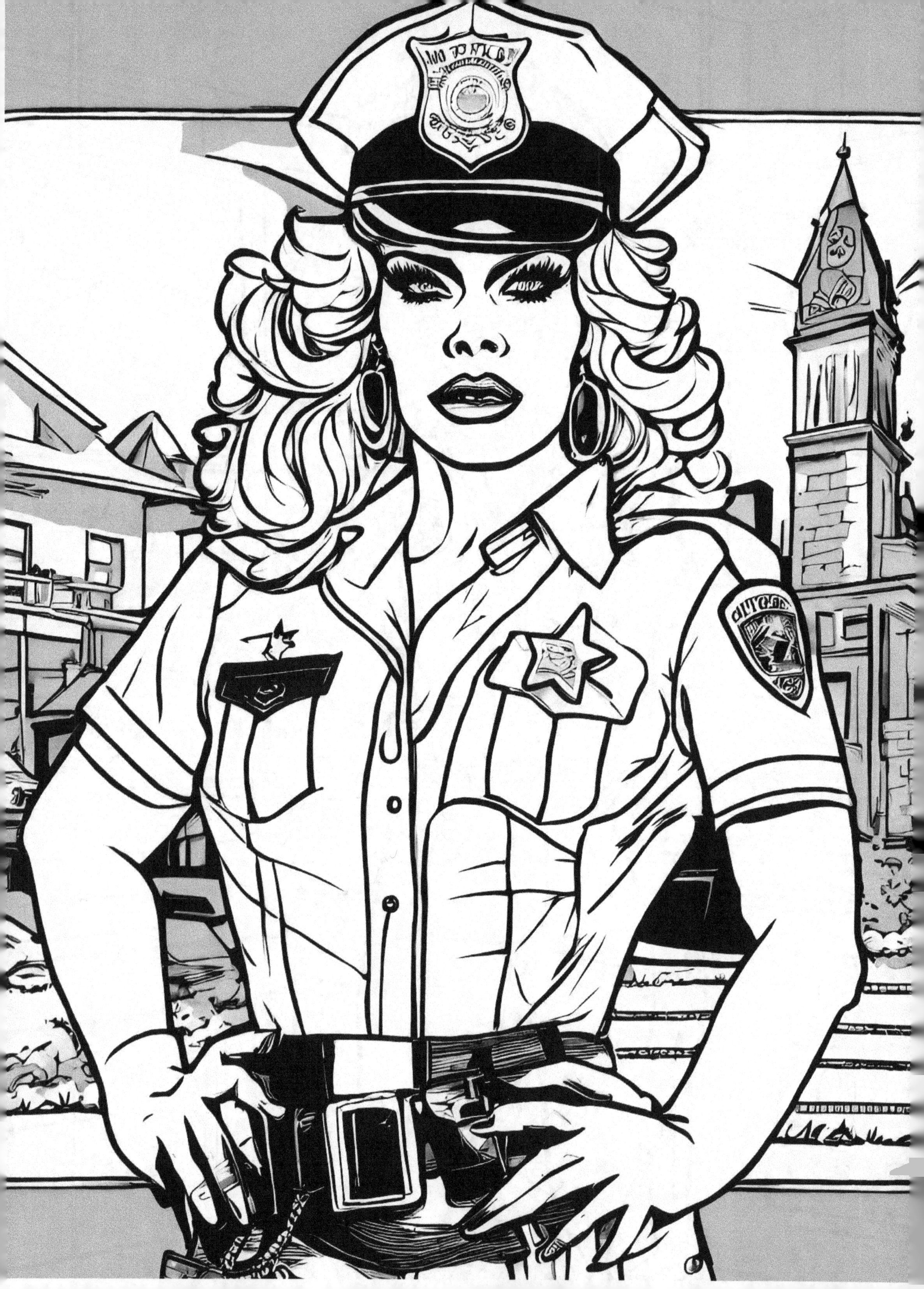

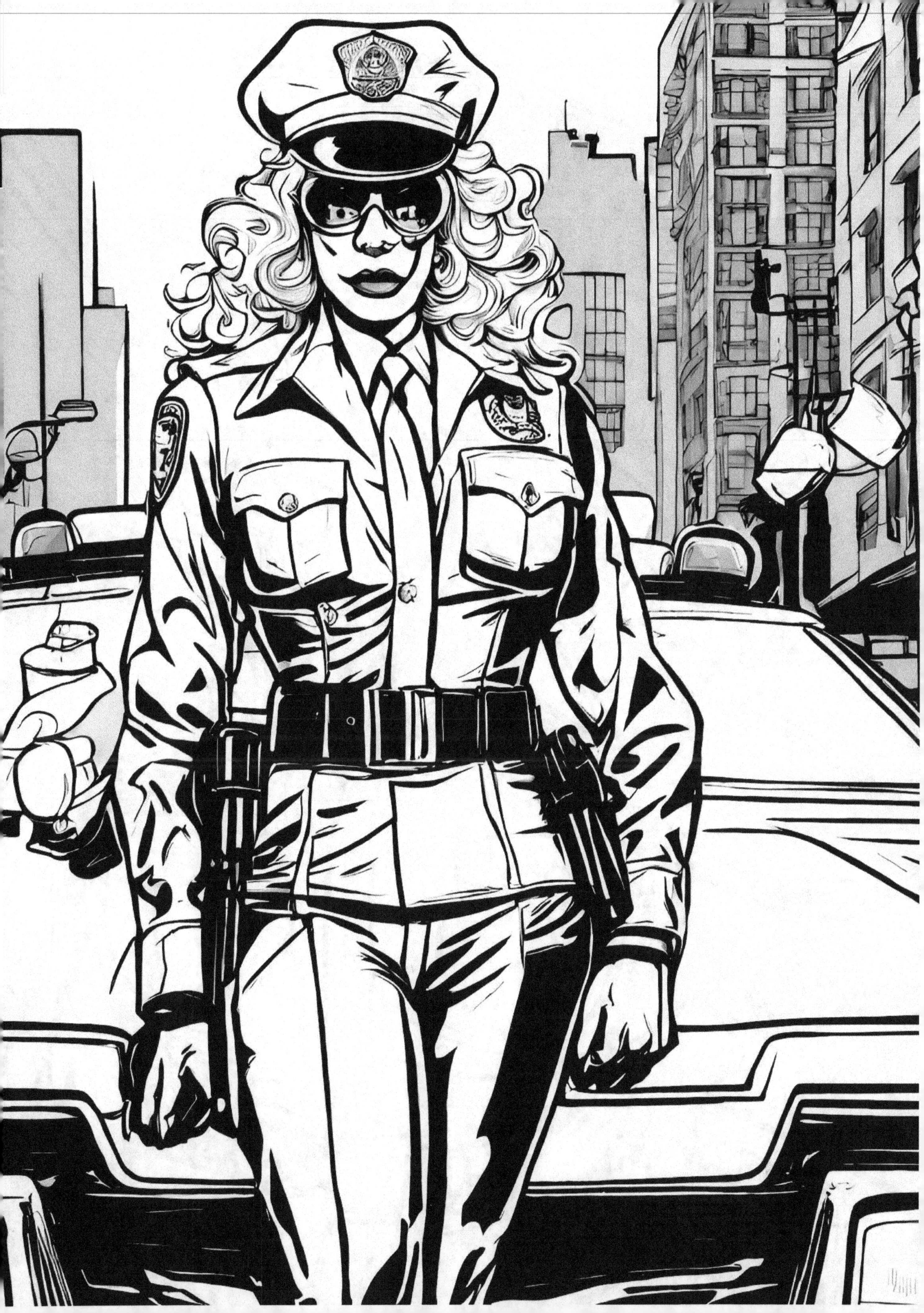

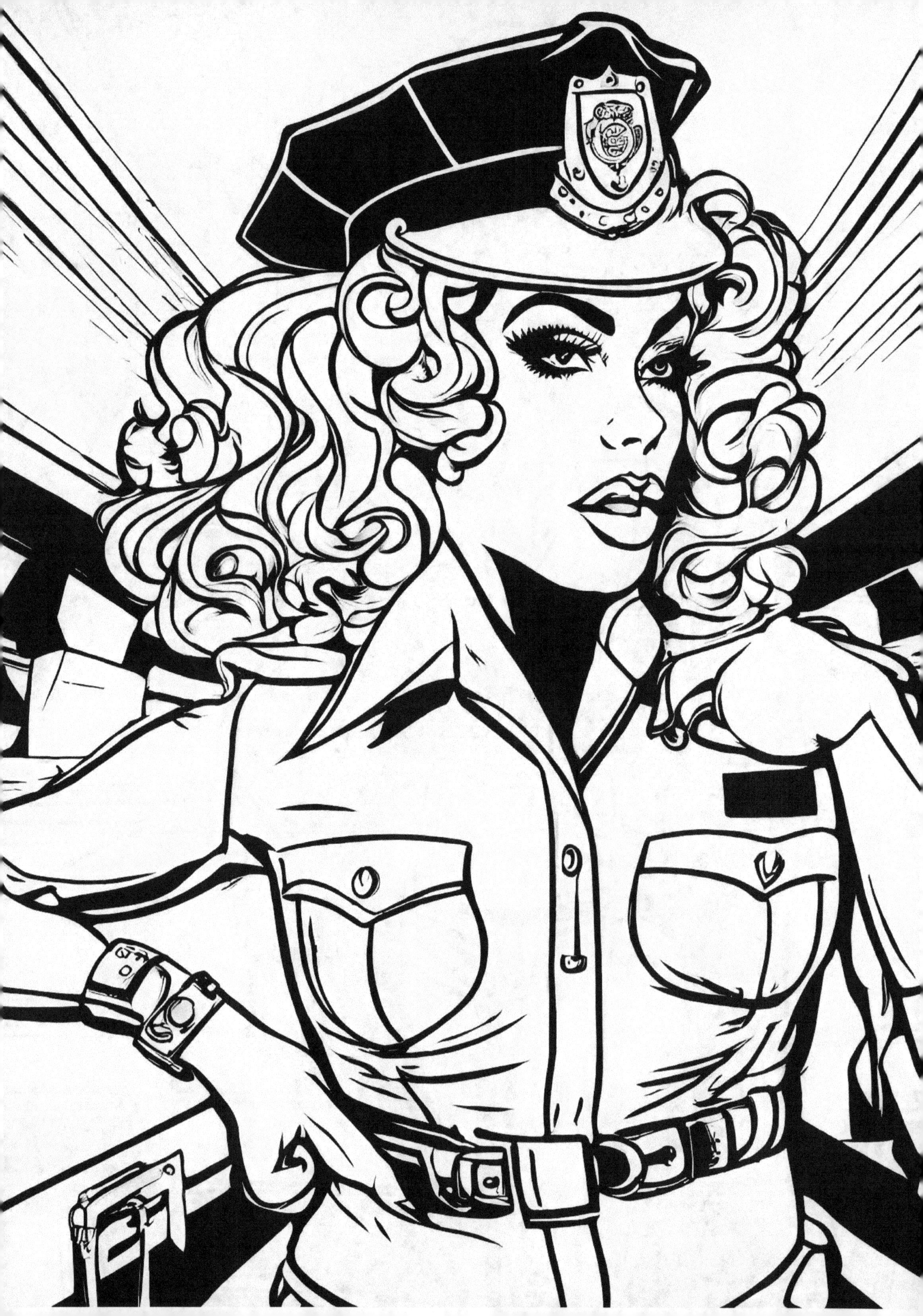

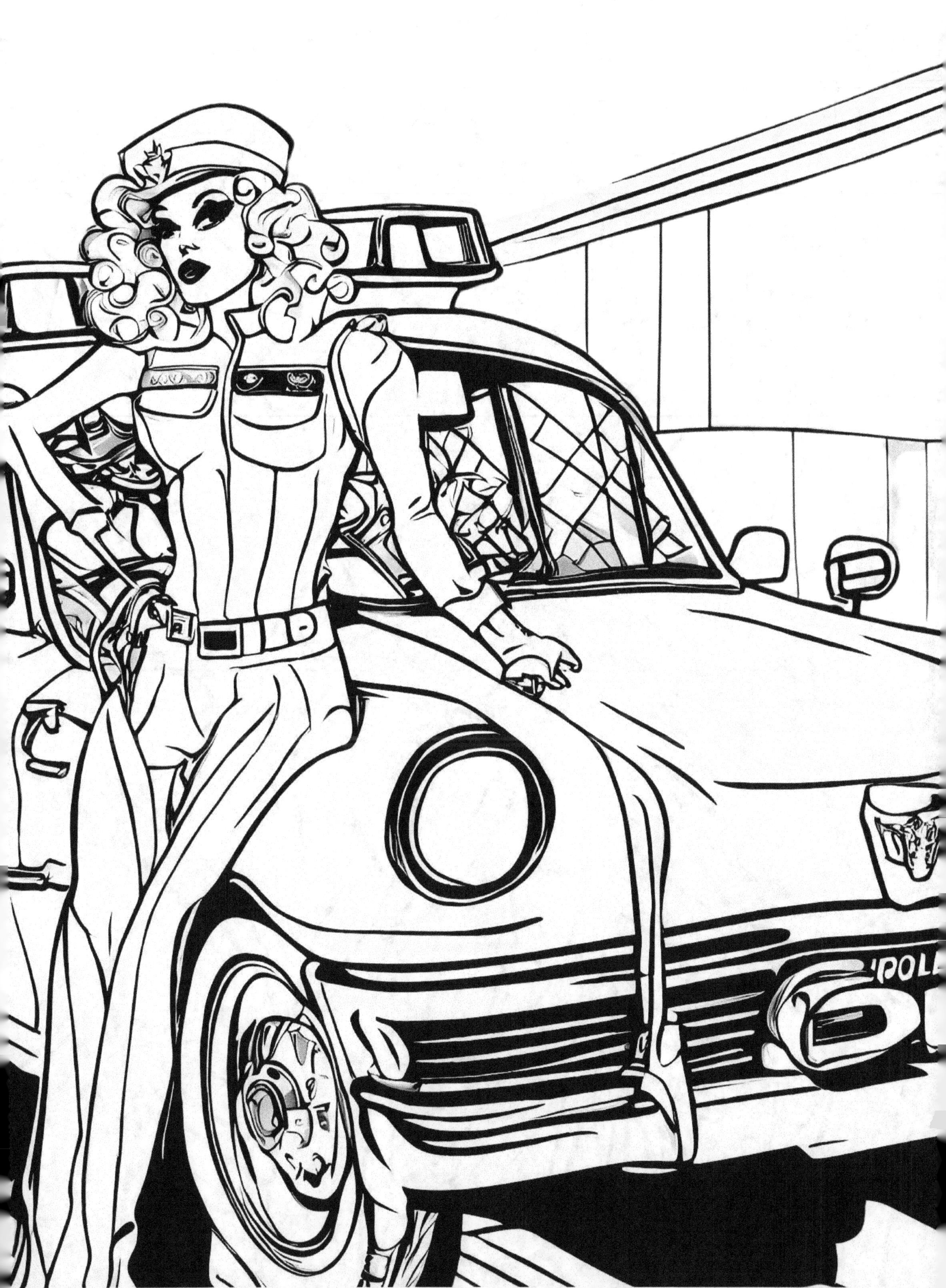

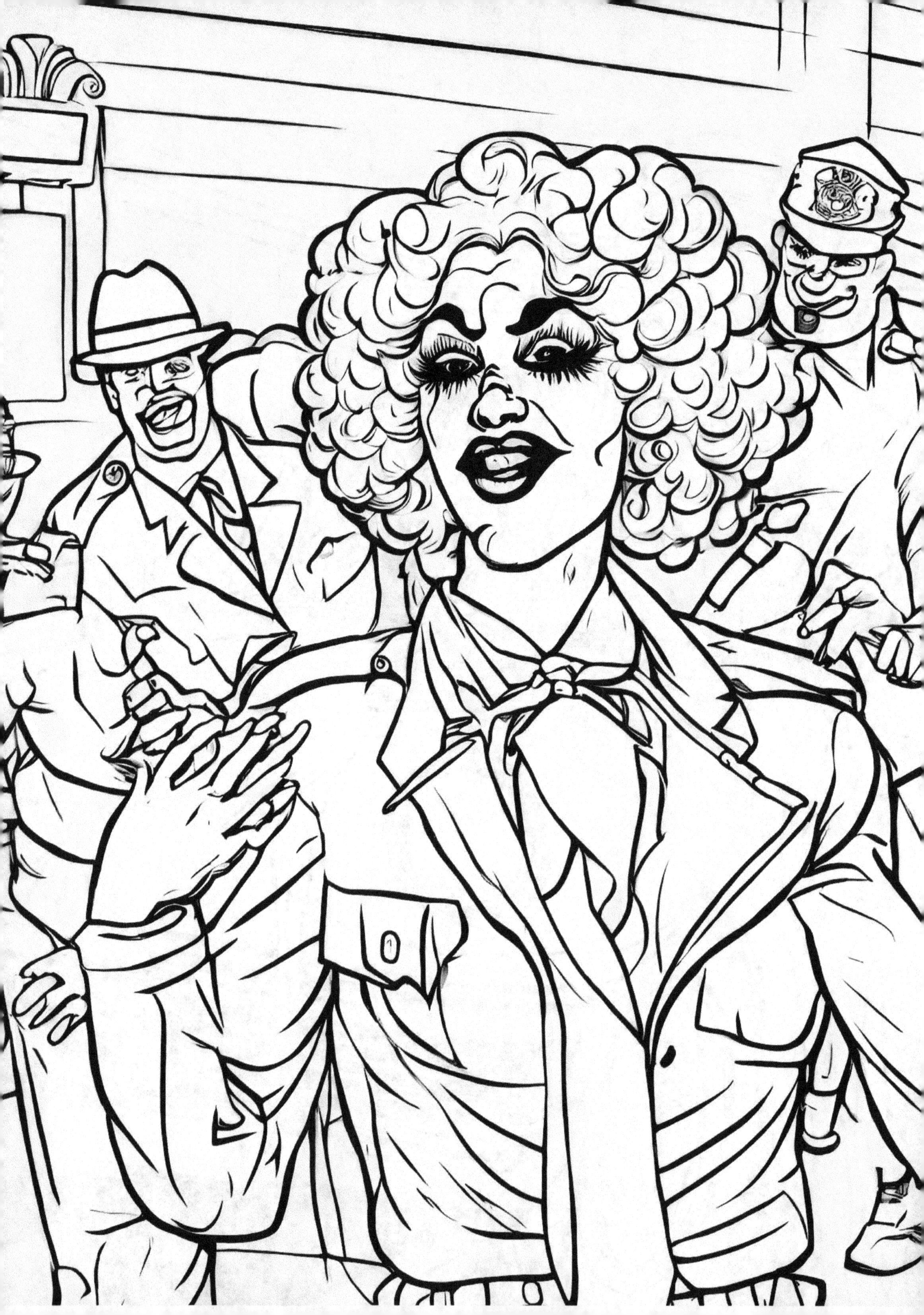

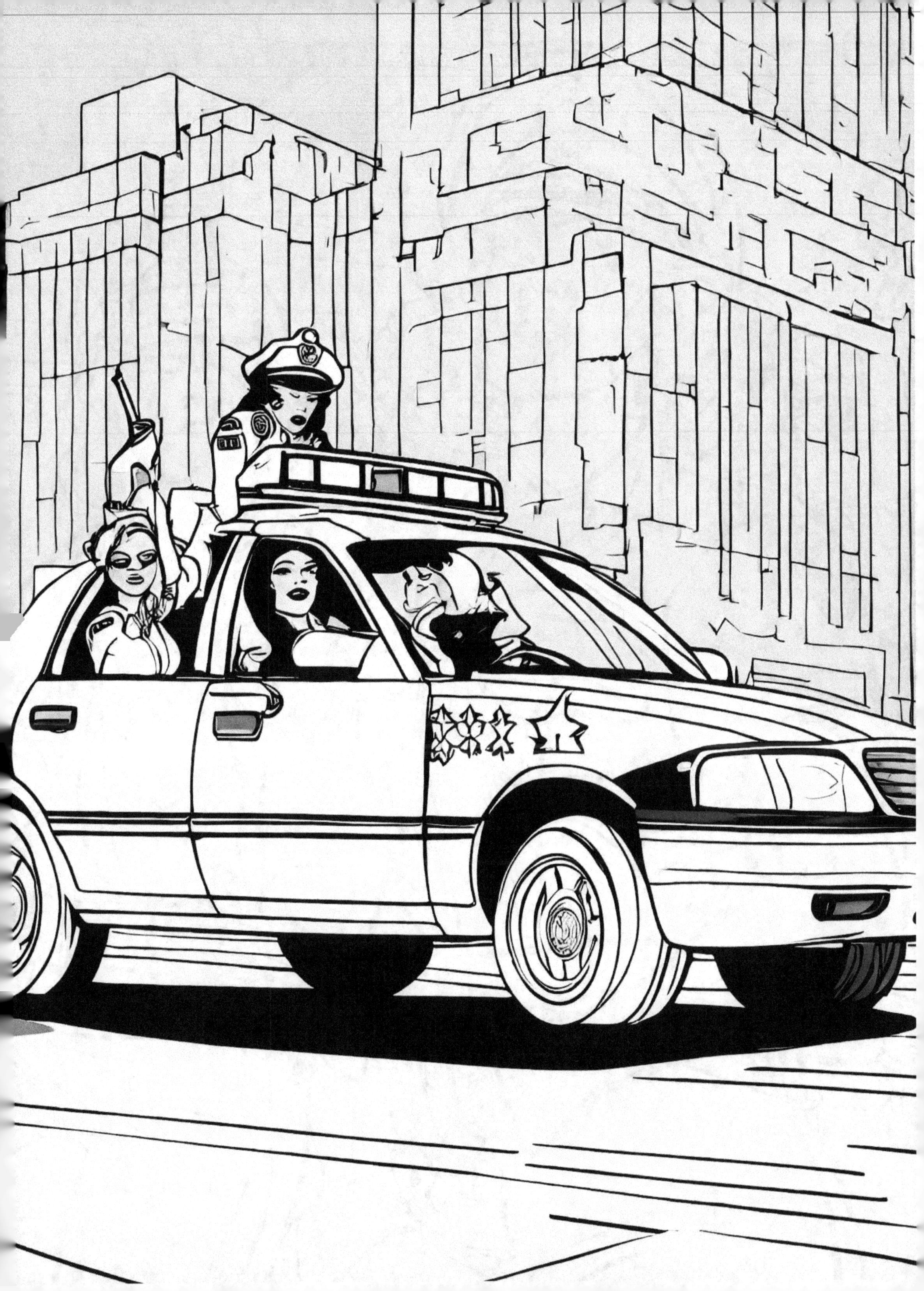

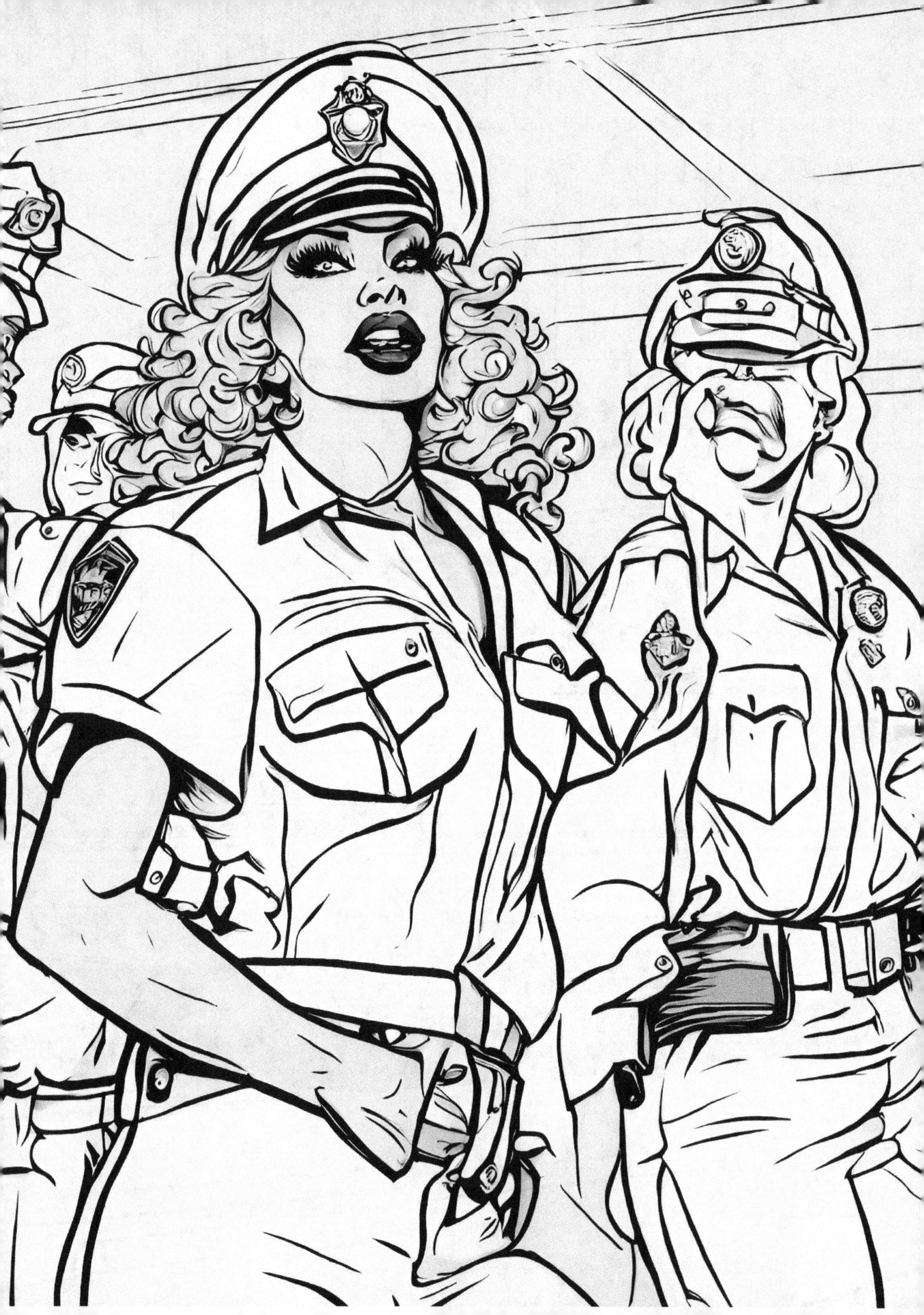

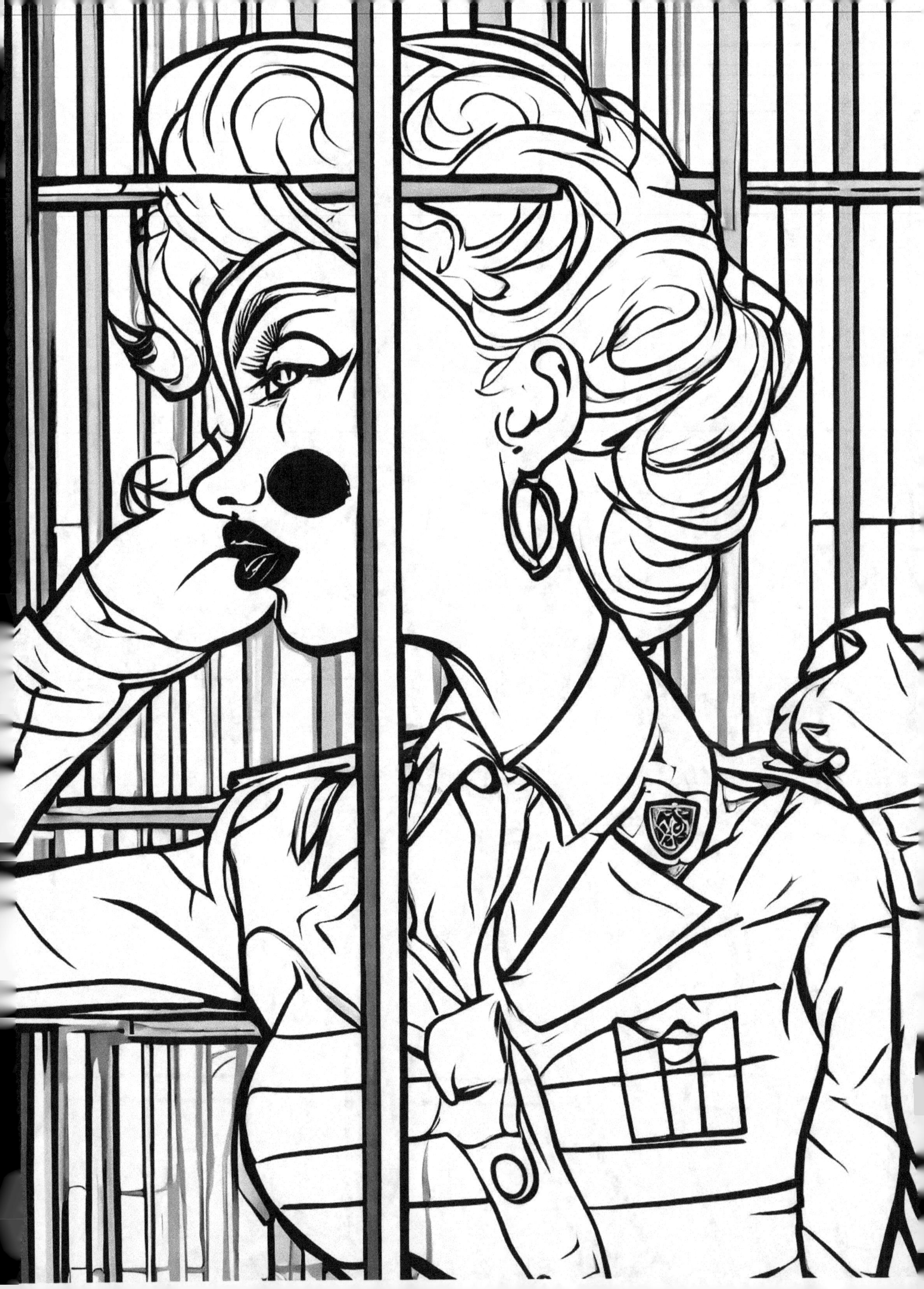

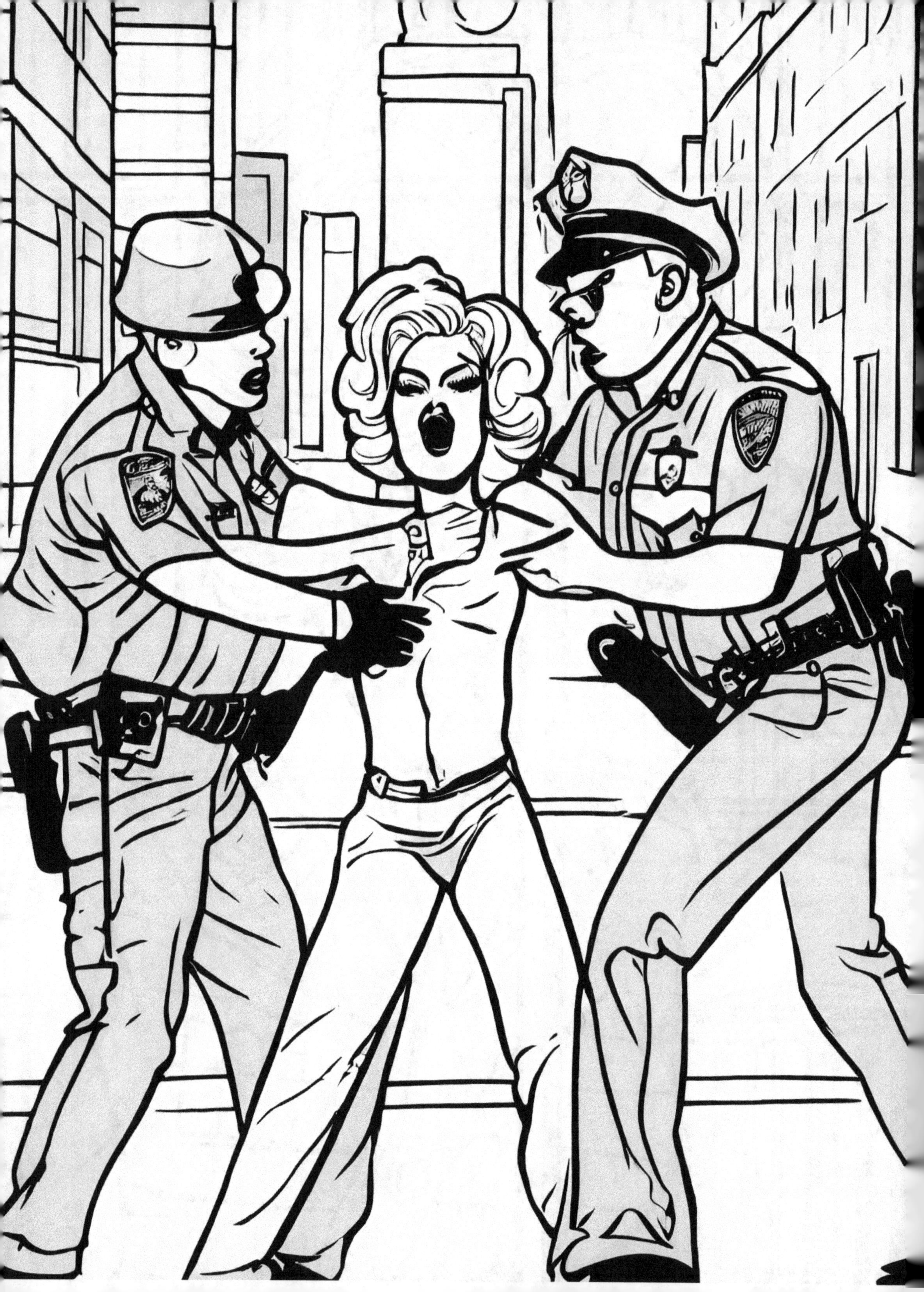

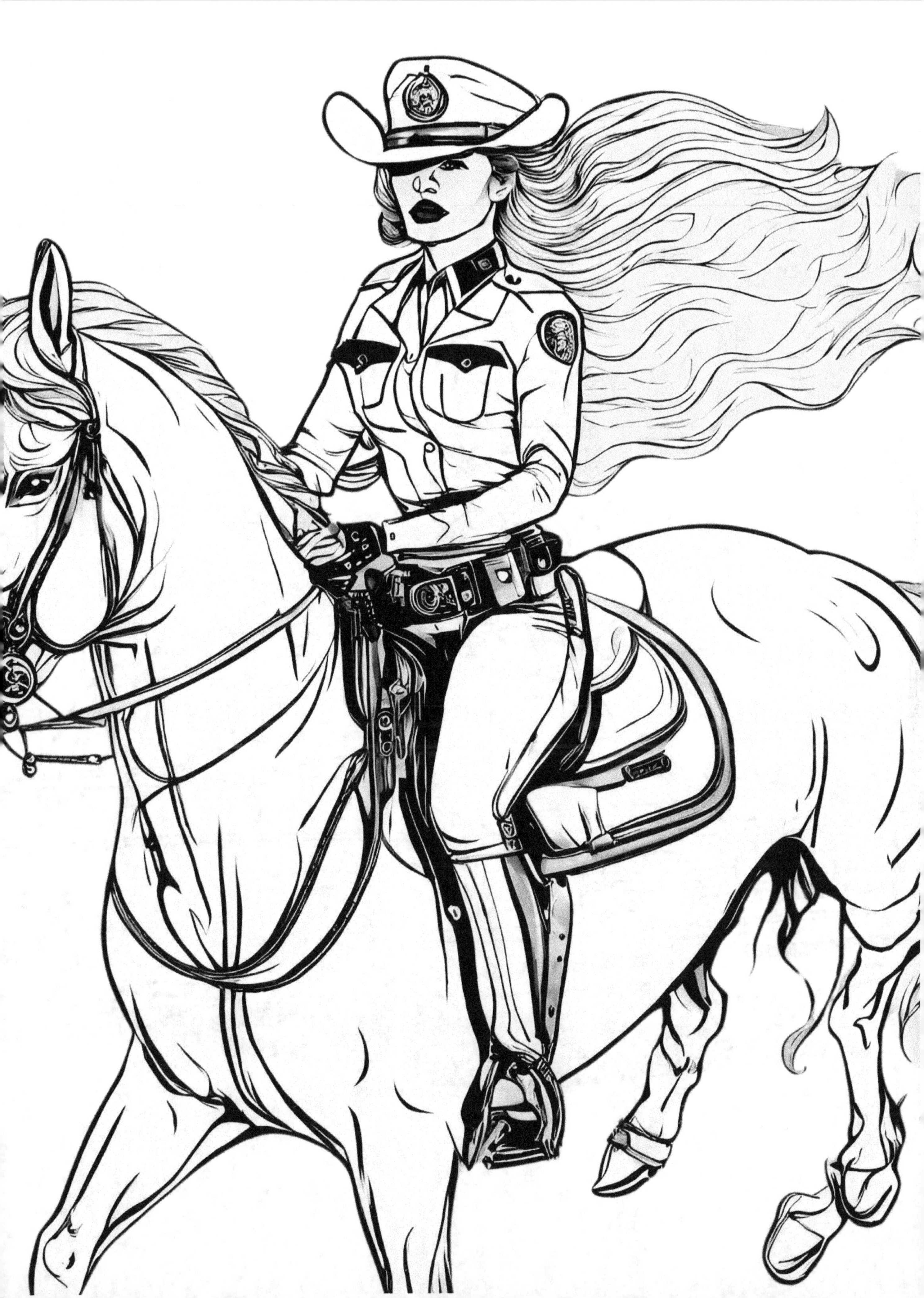

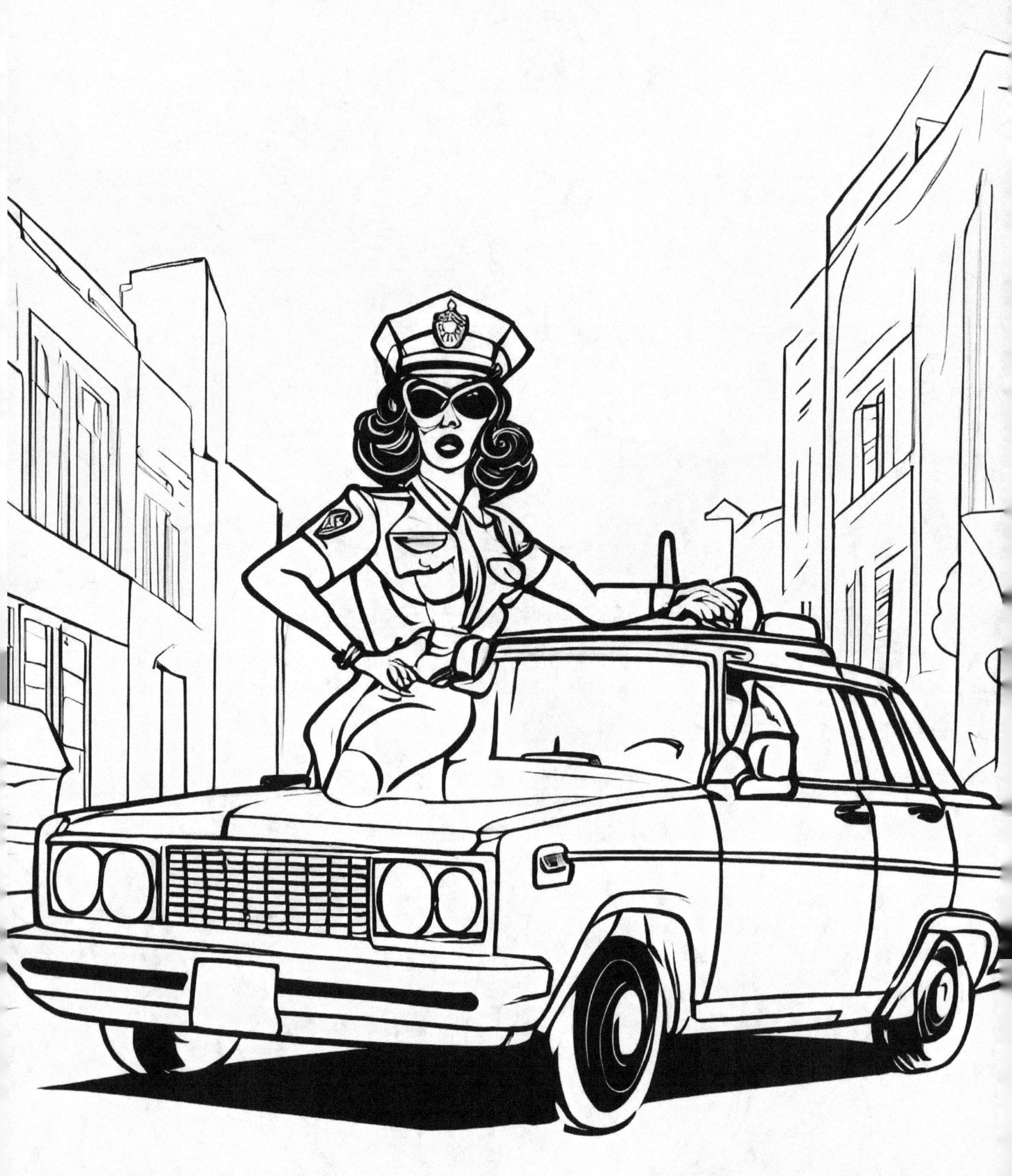

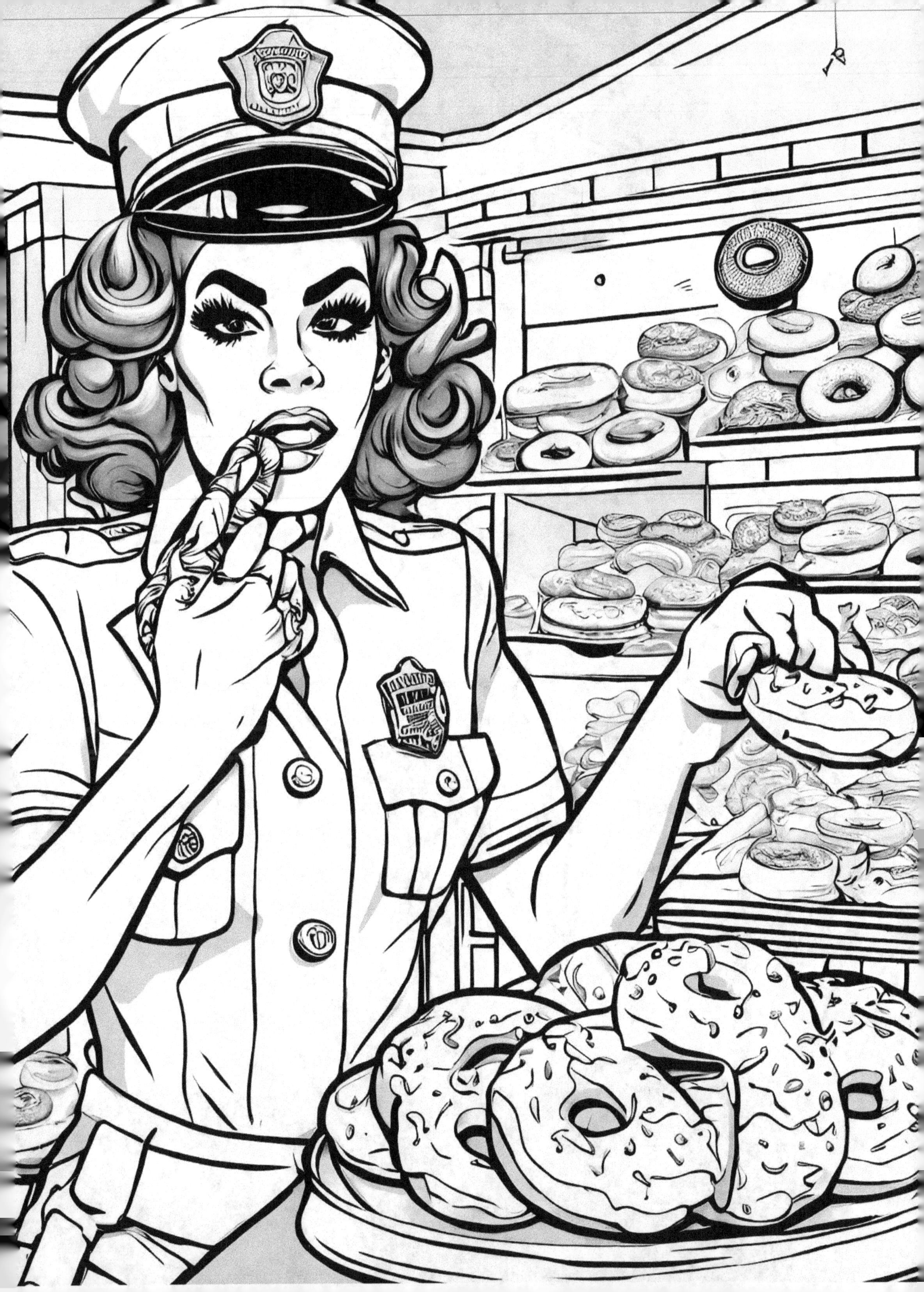

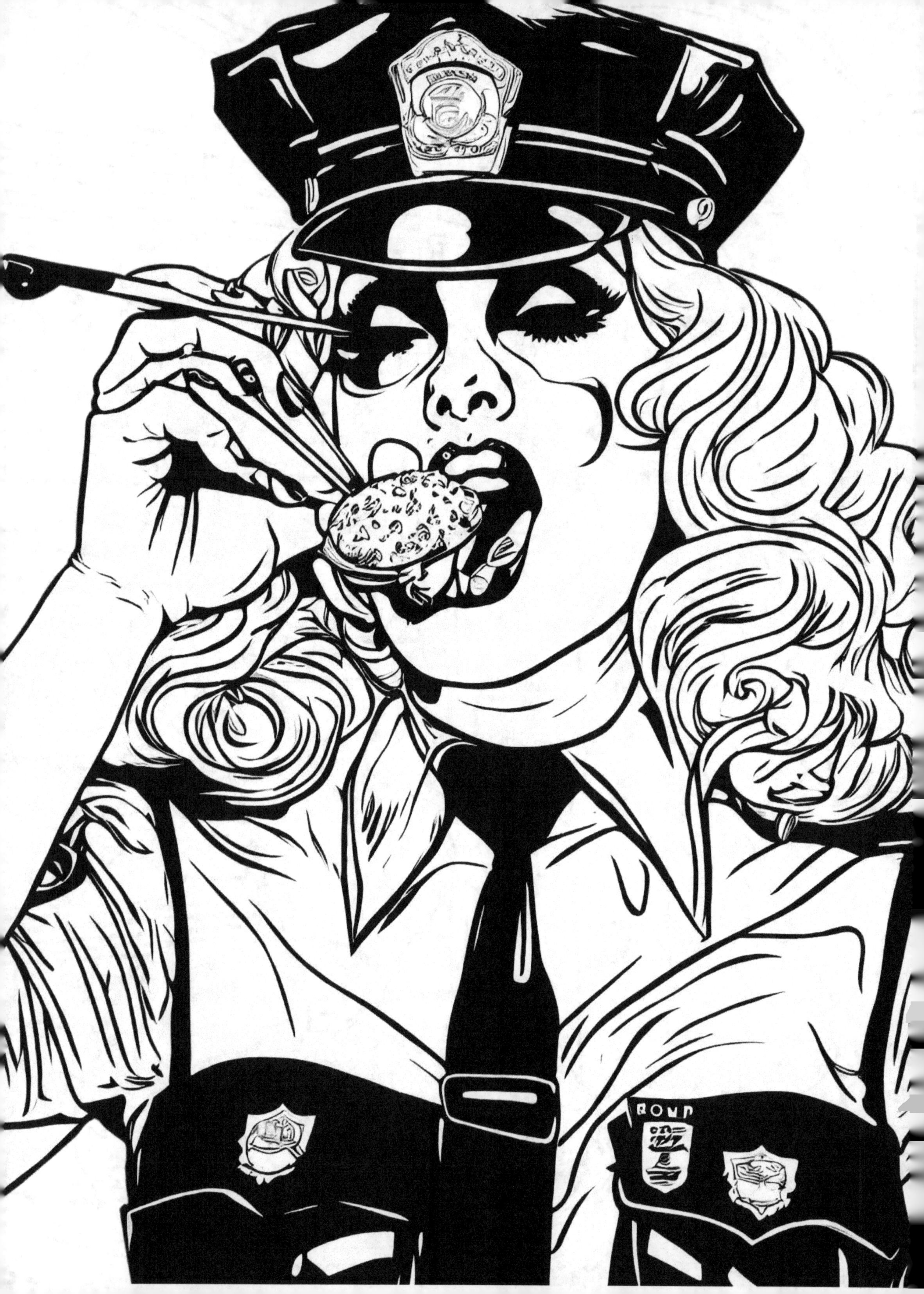

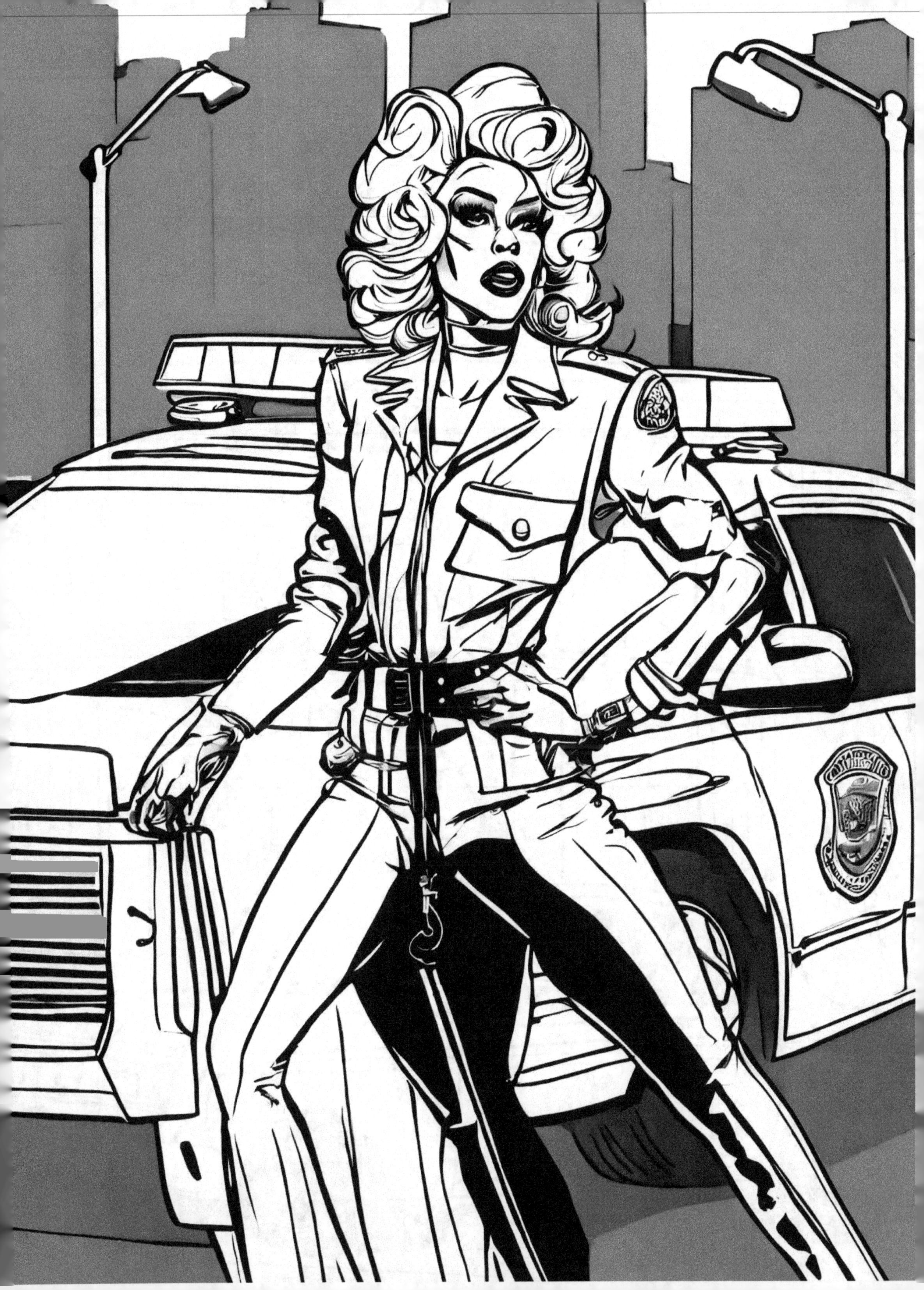

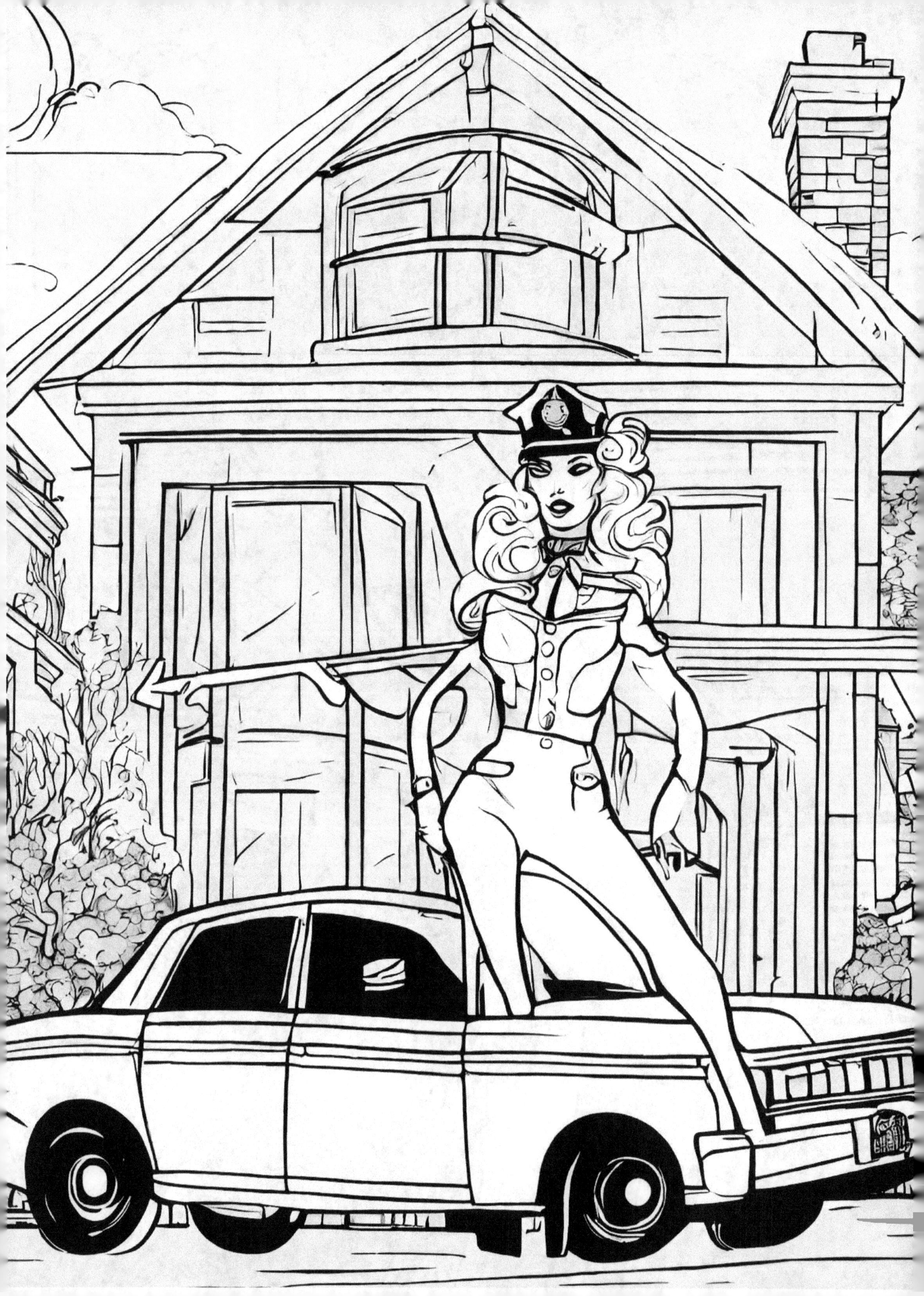

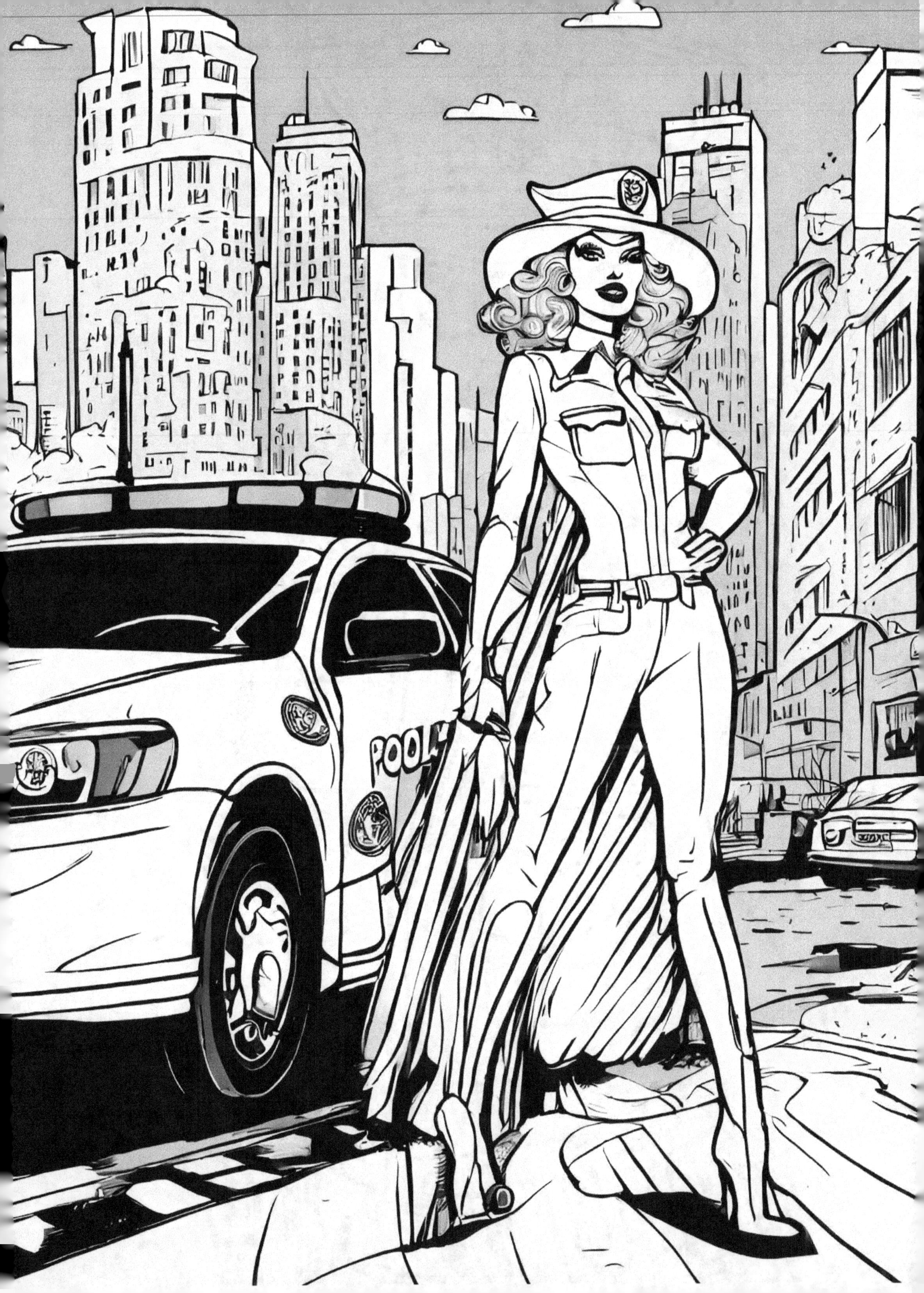
POOL

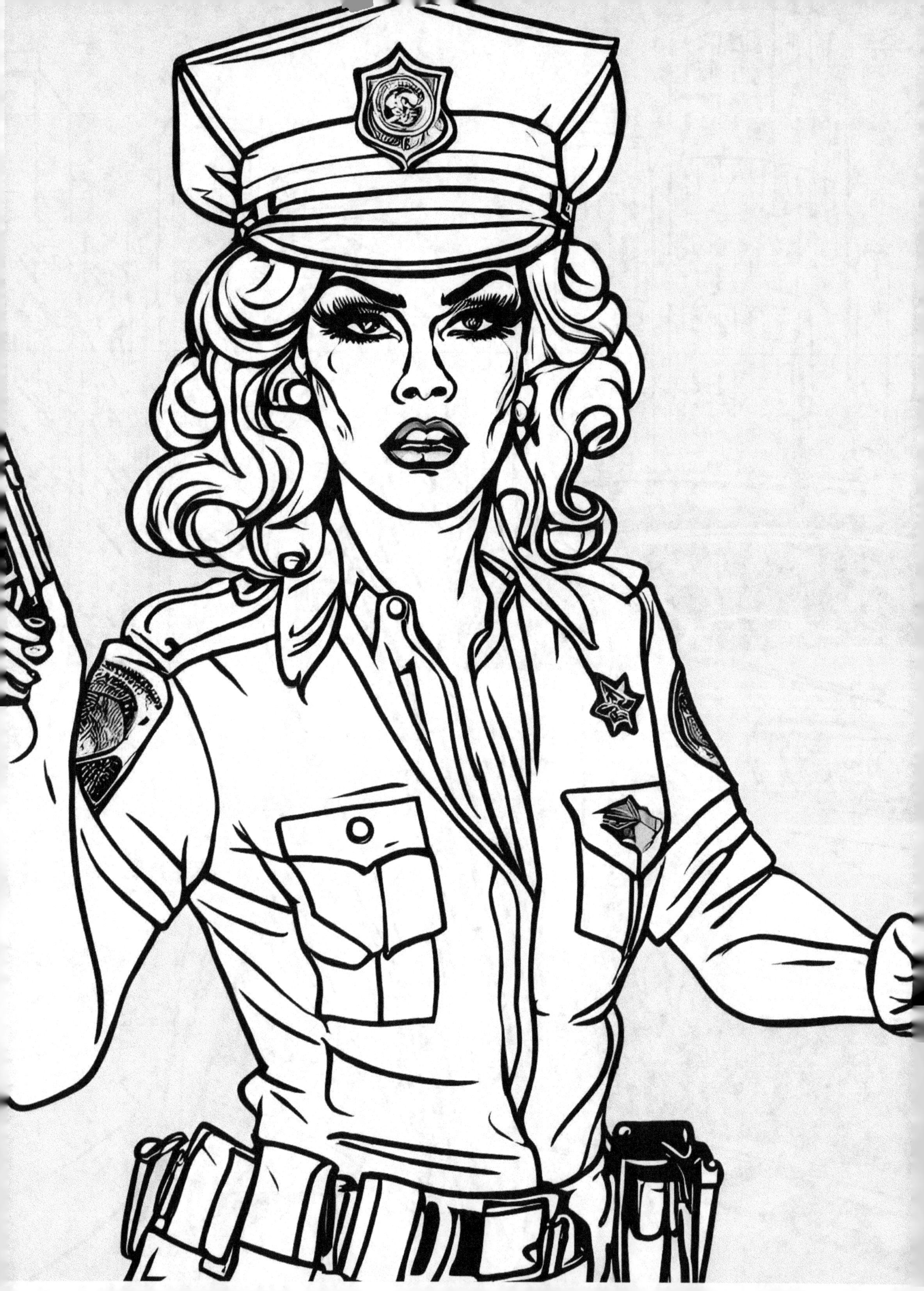

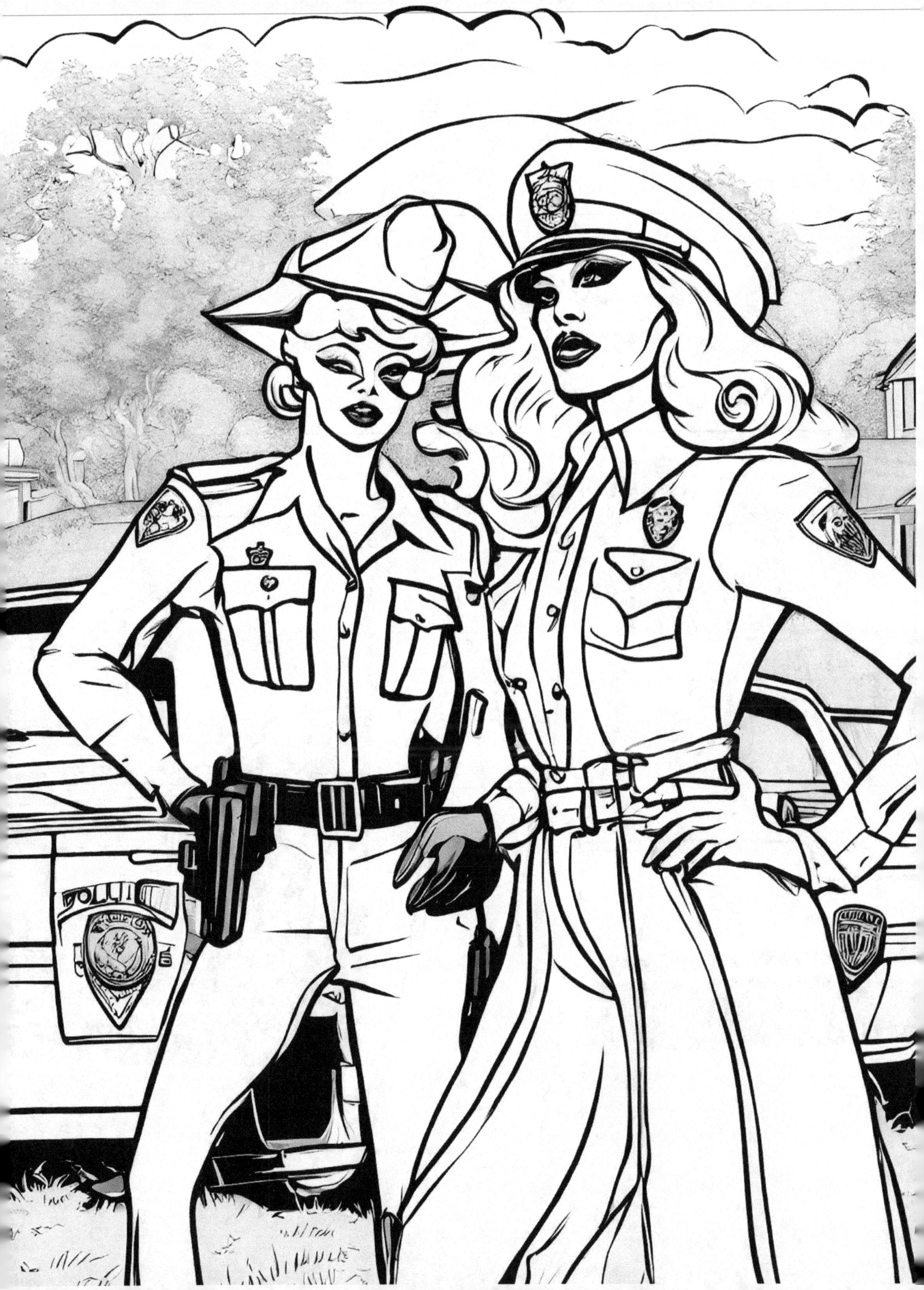

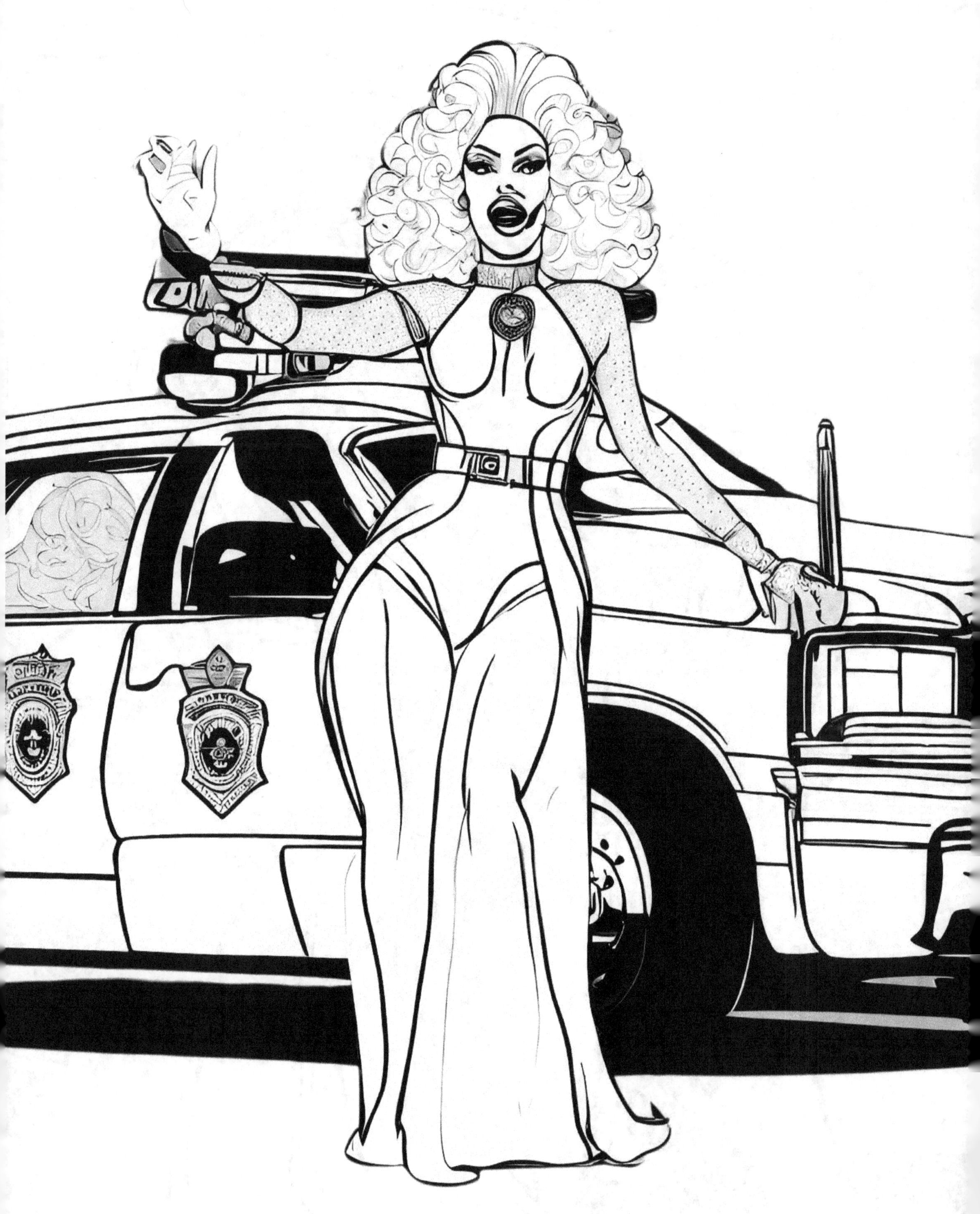

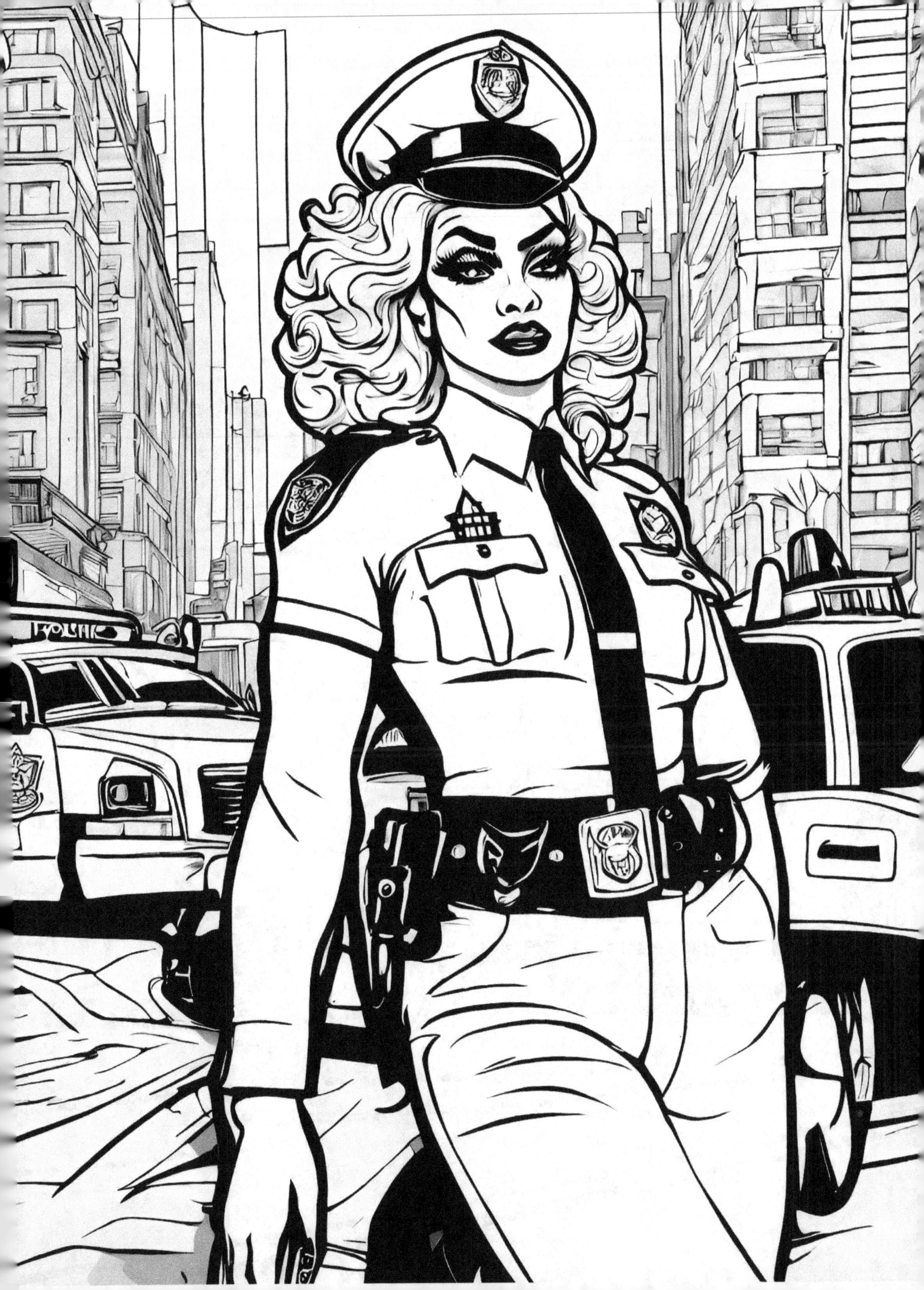

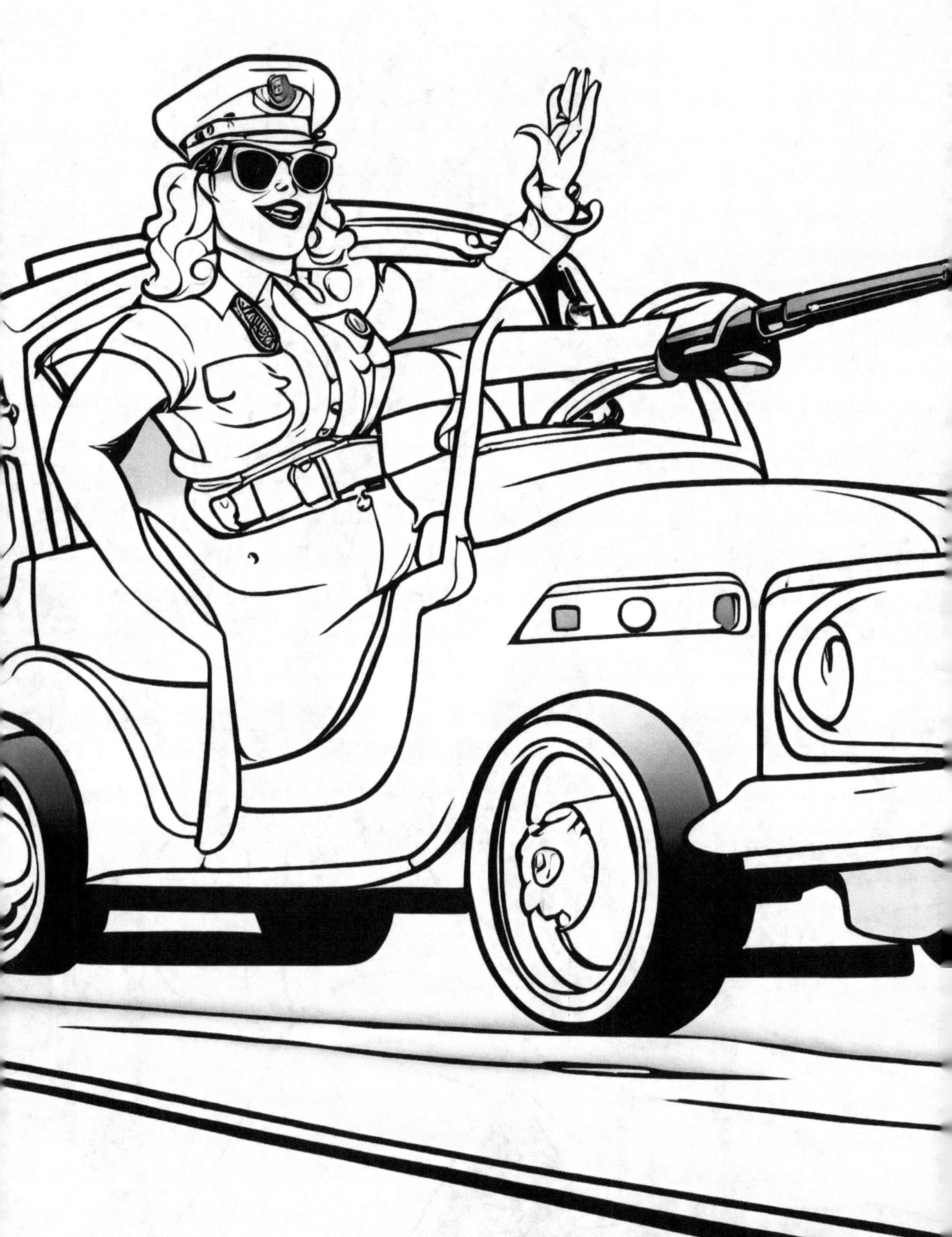

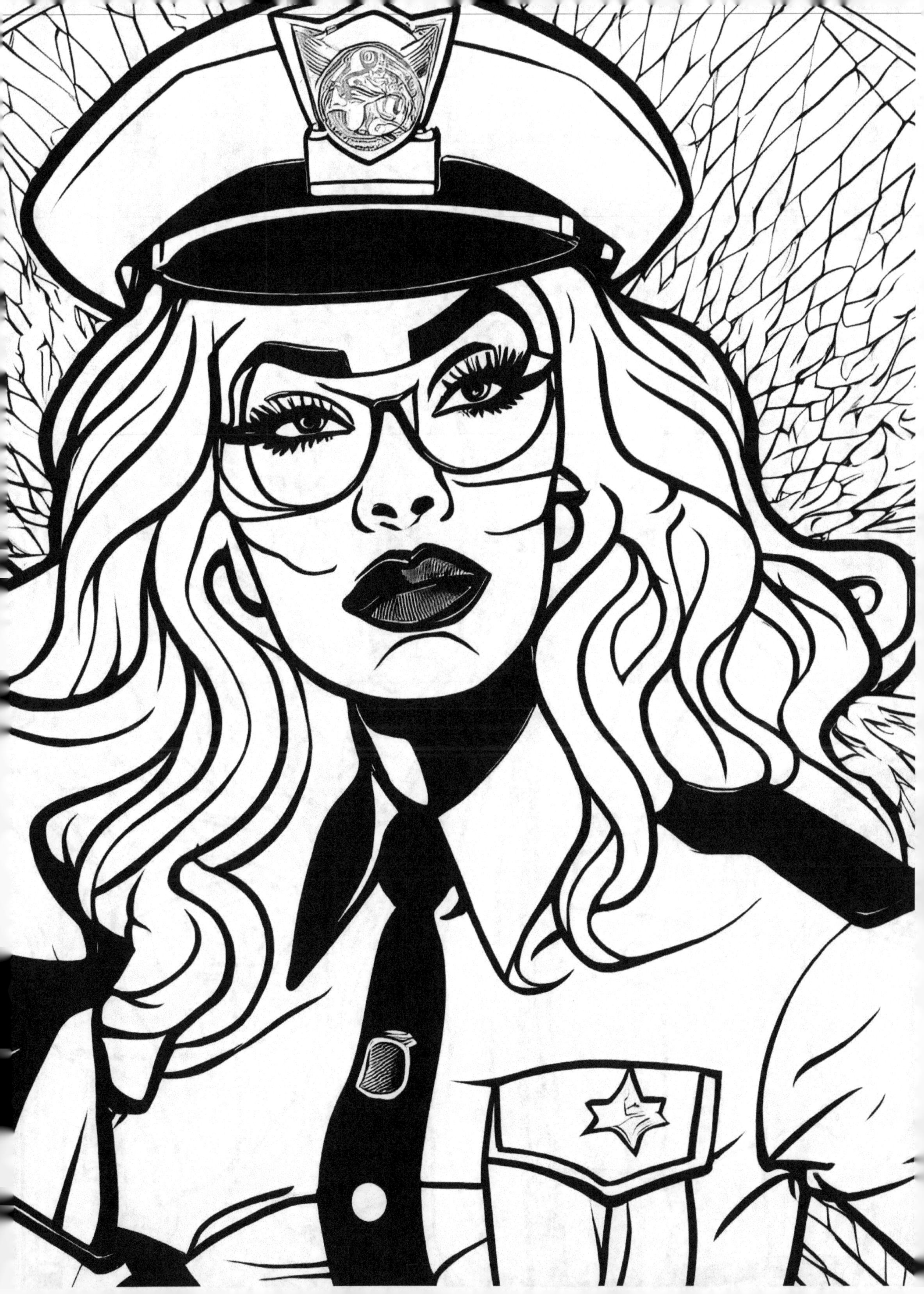

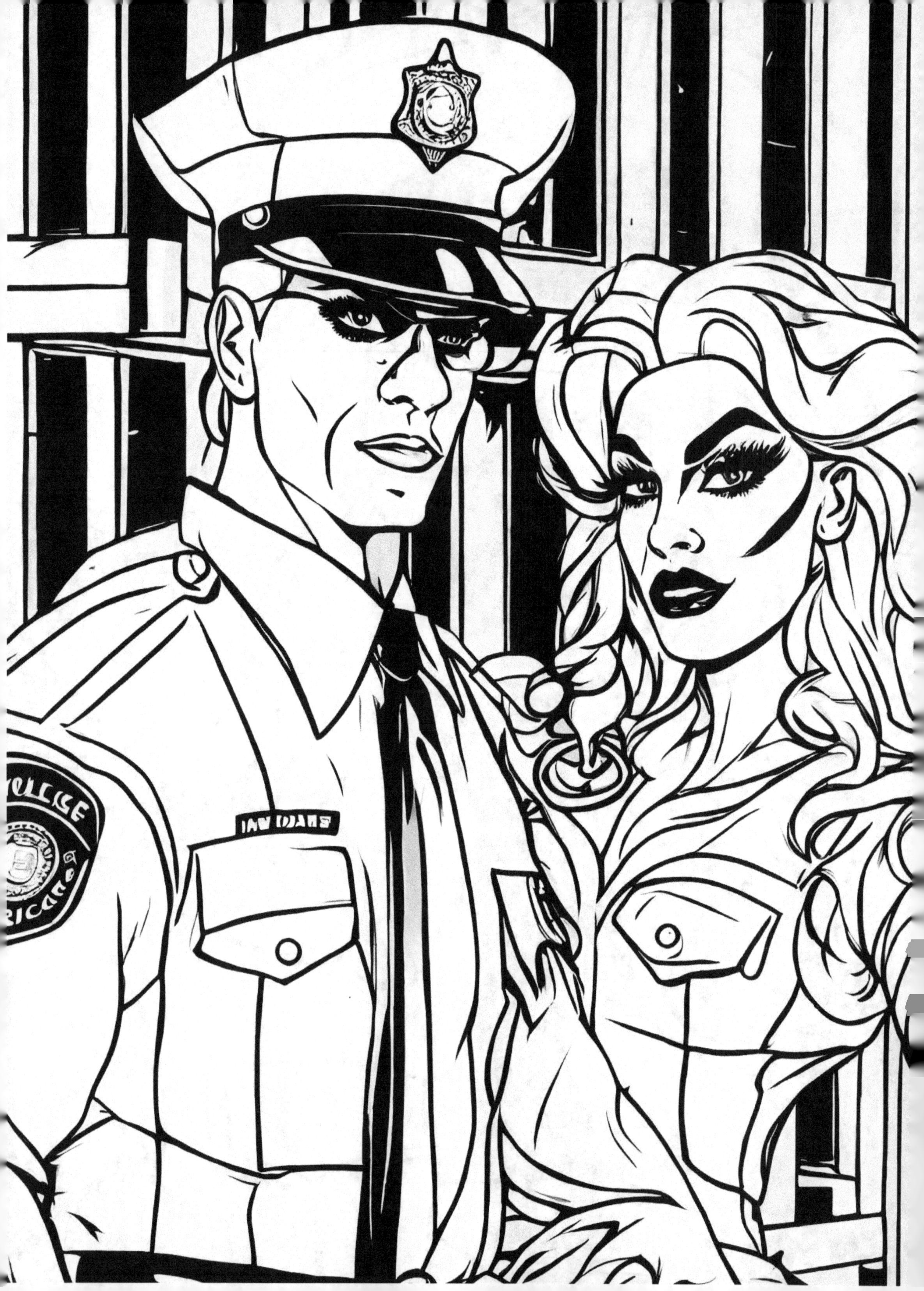

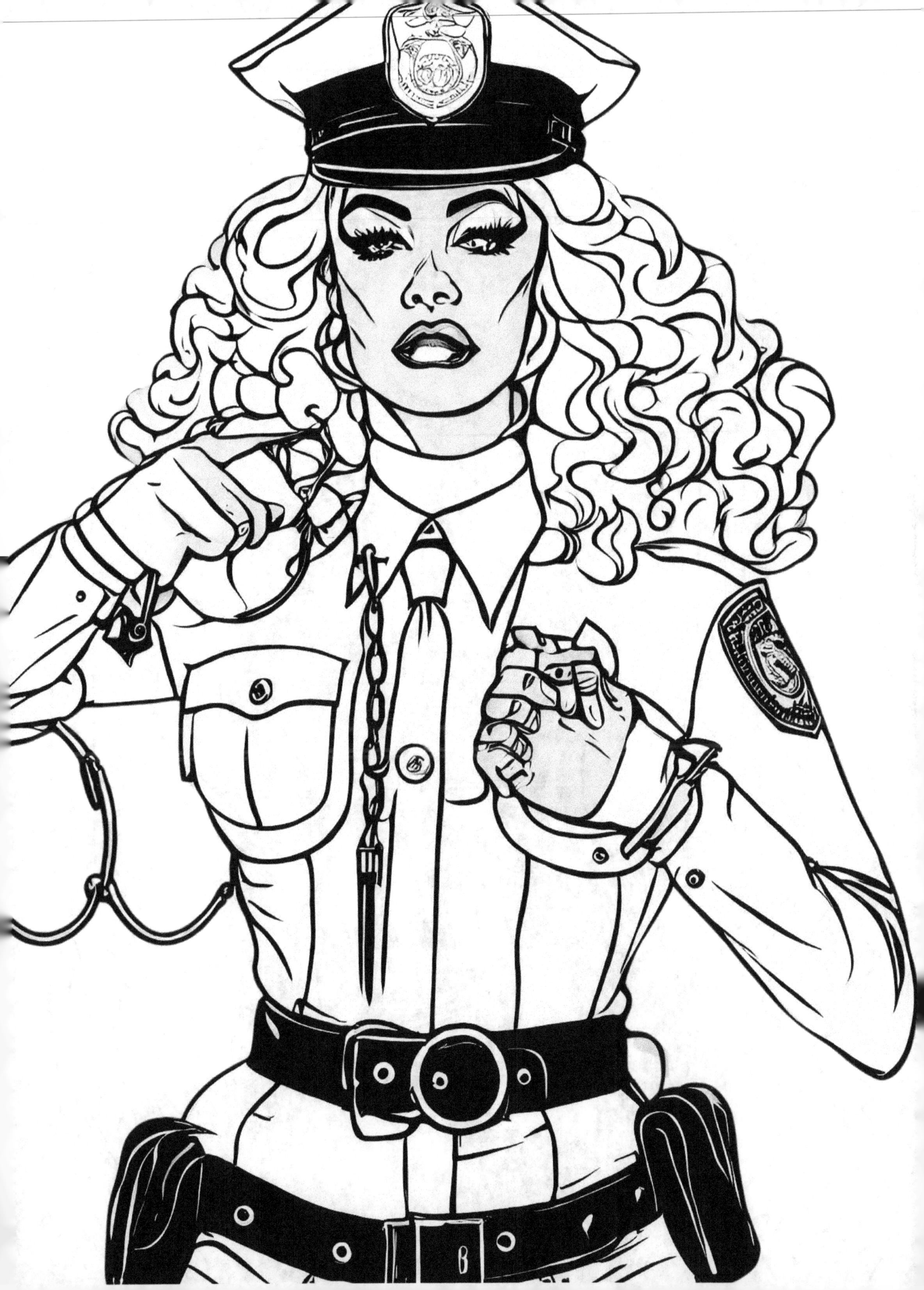

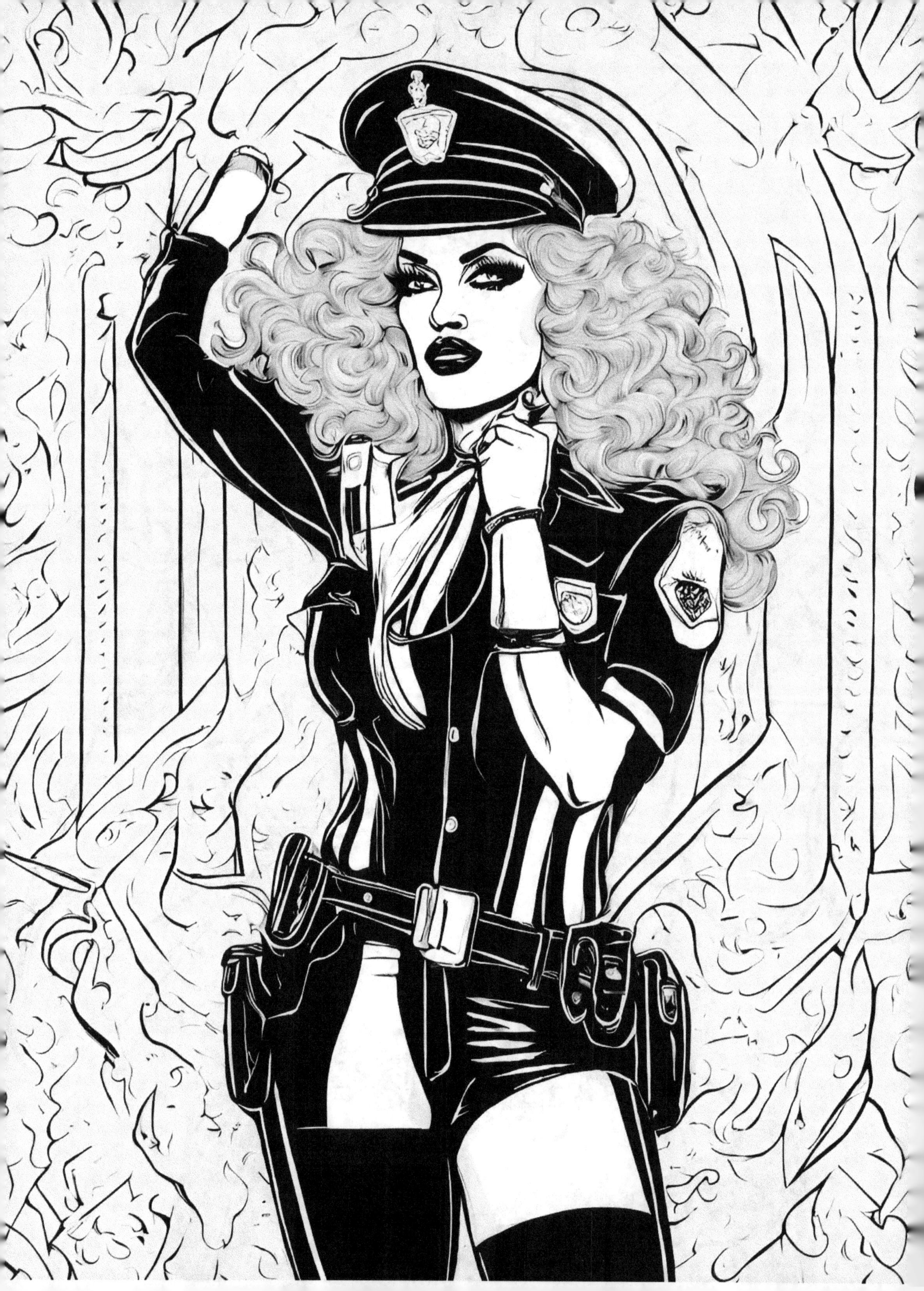

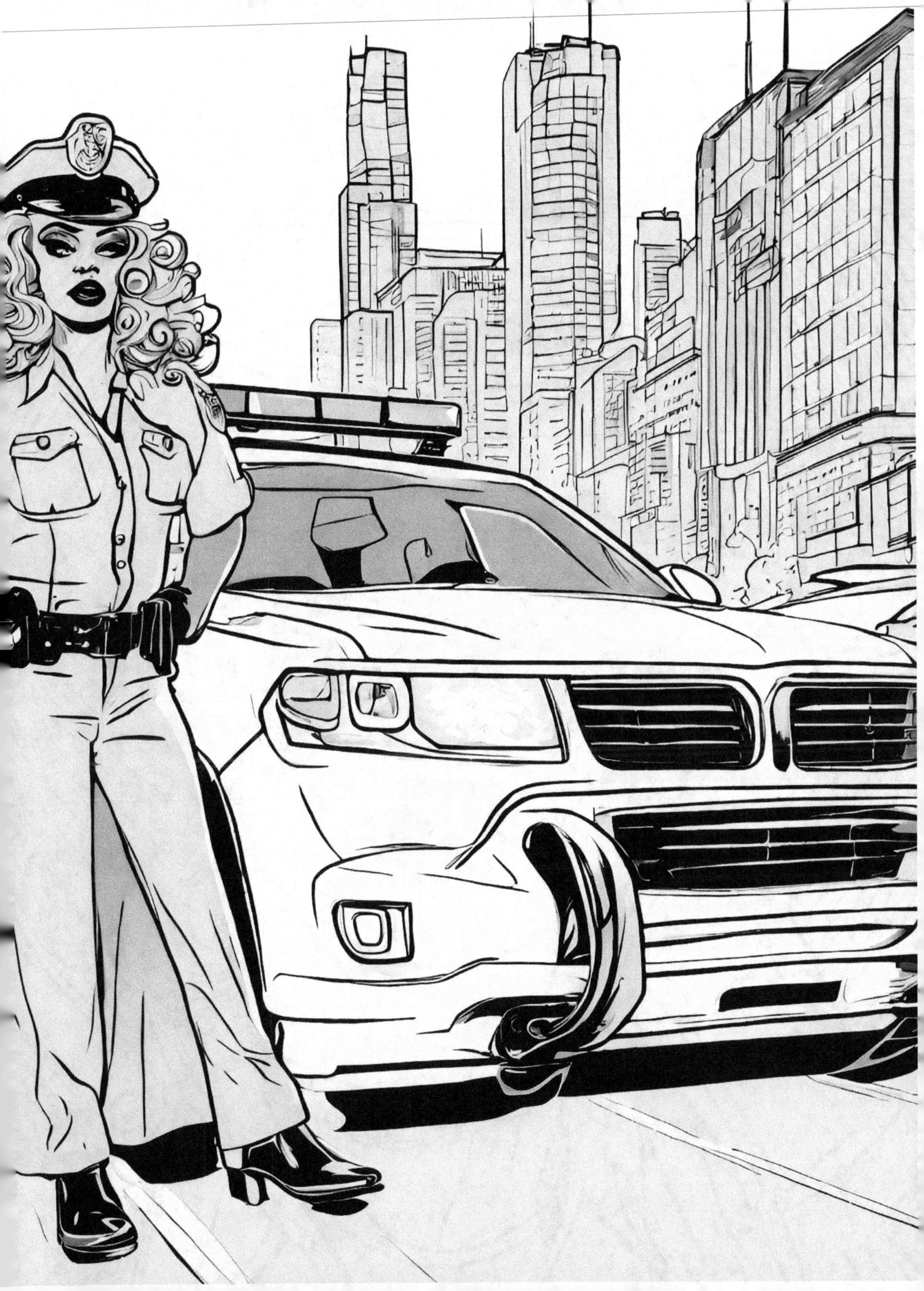

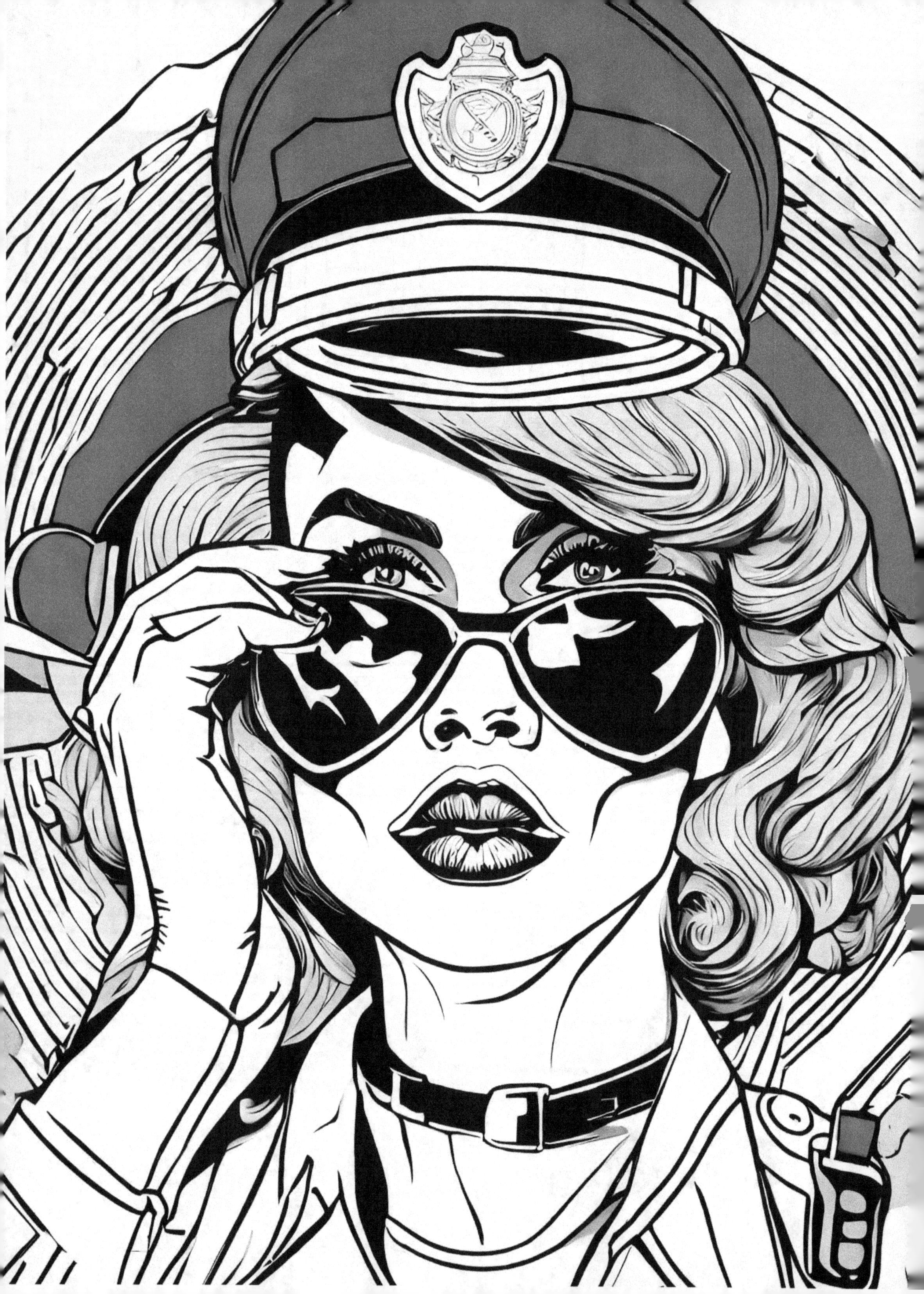

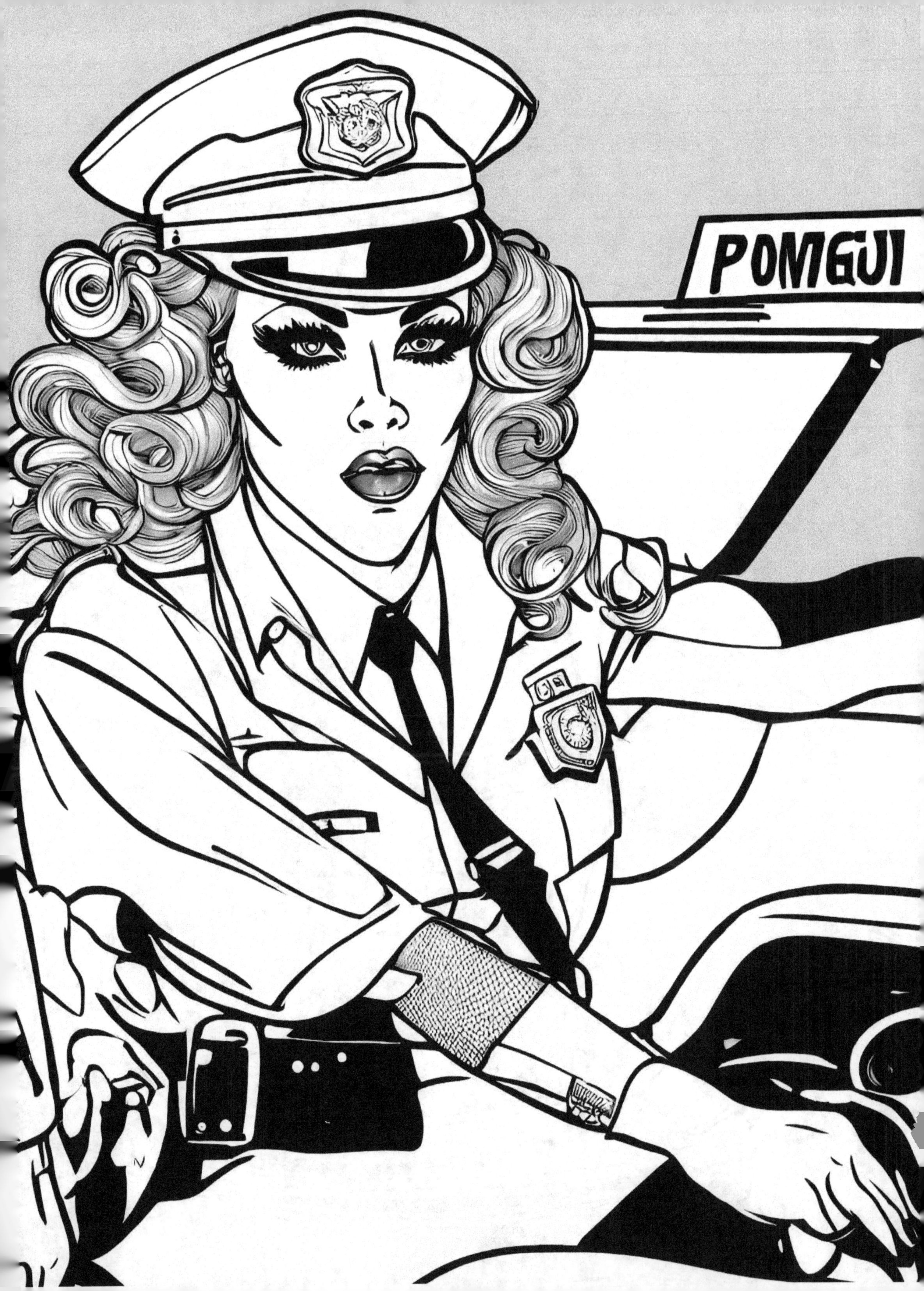
POMGUI

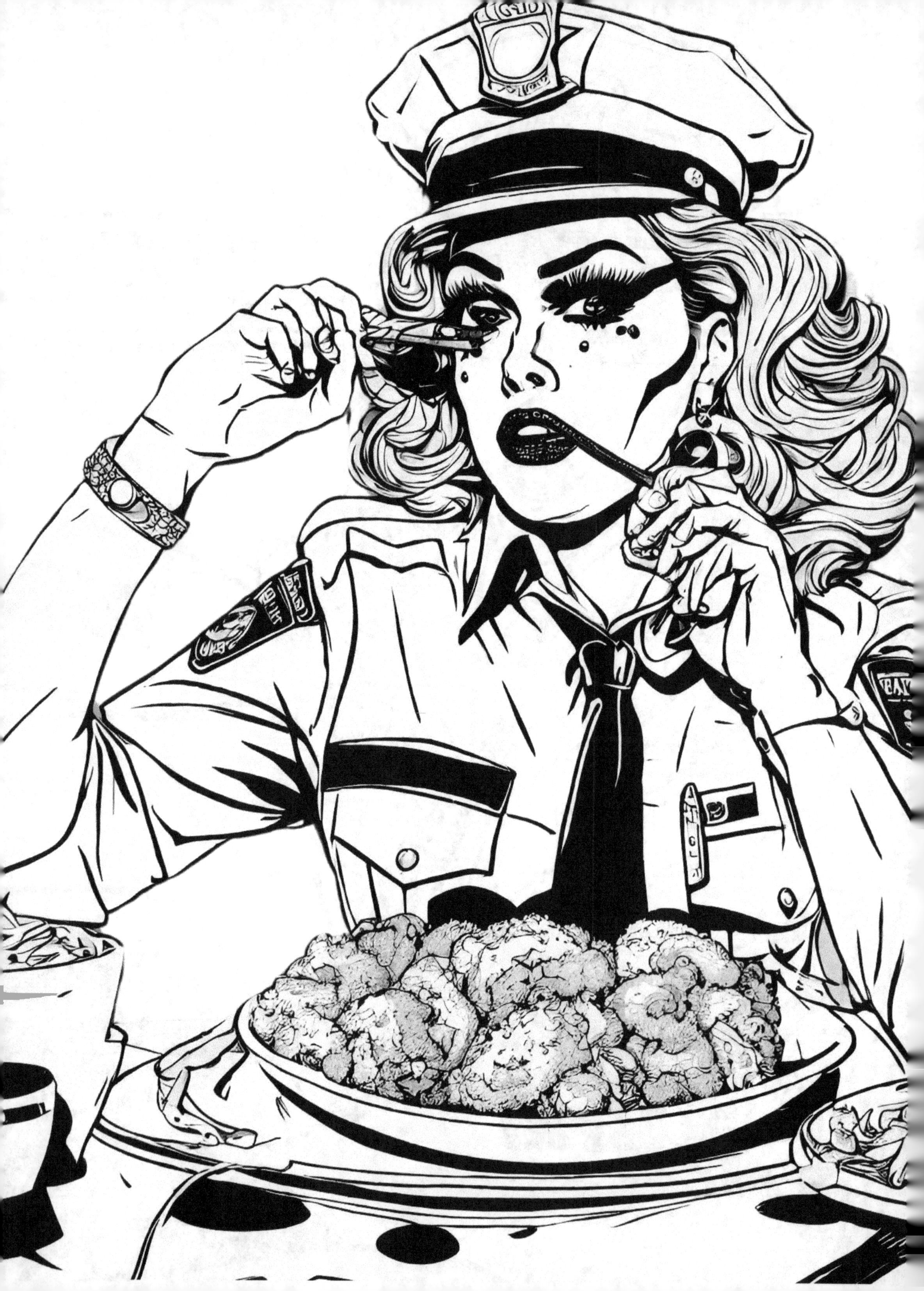

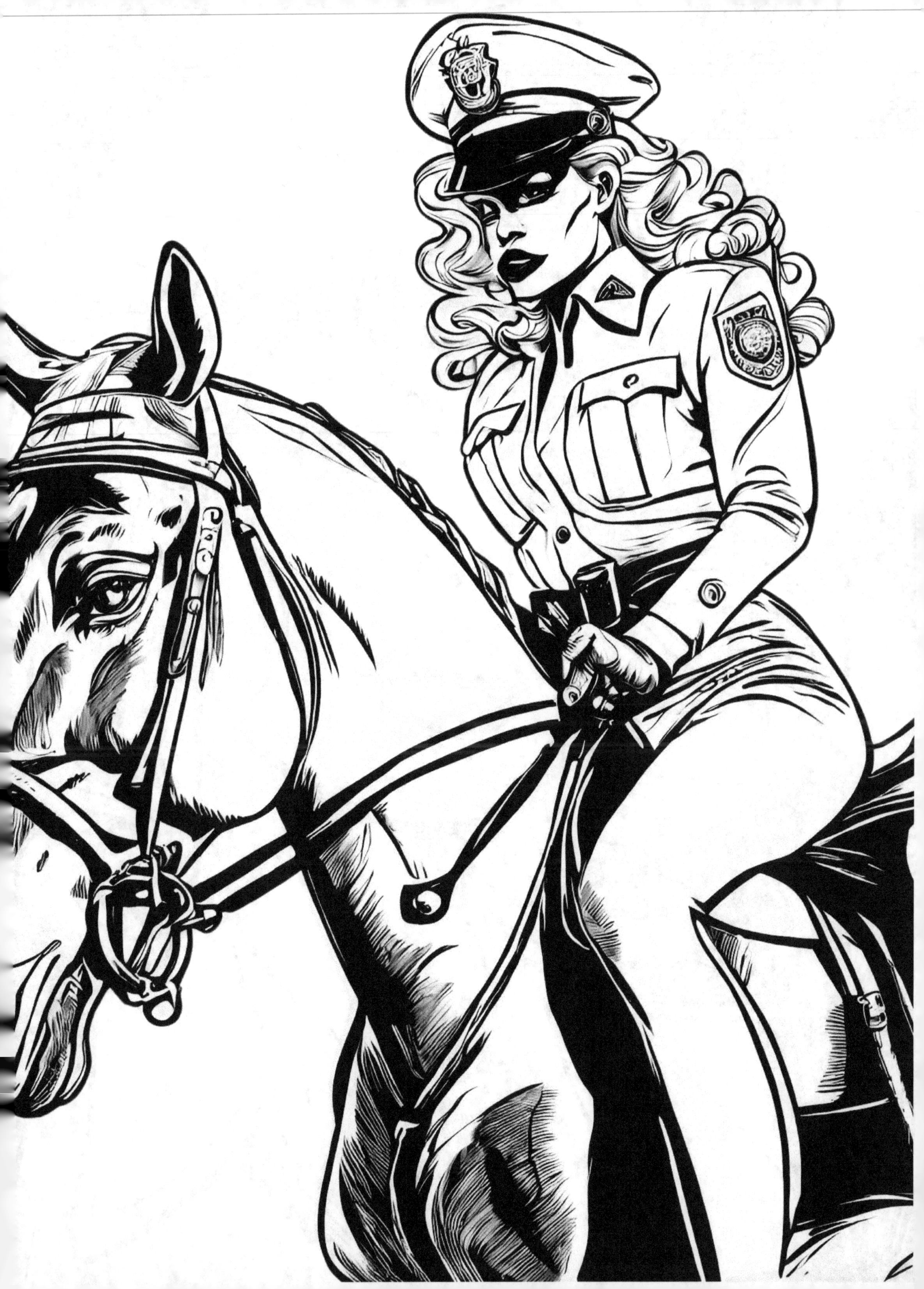

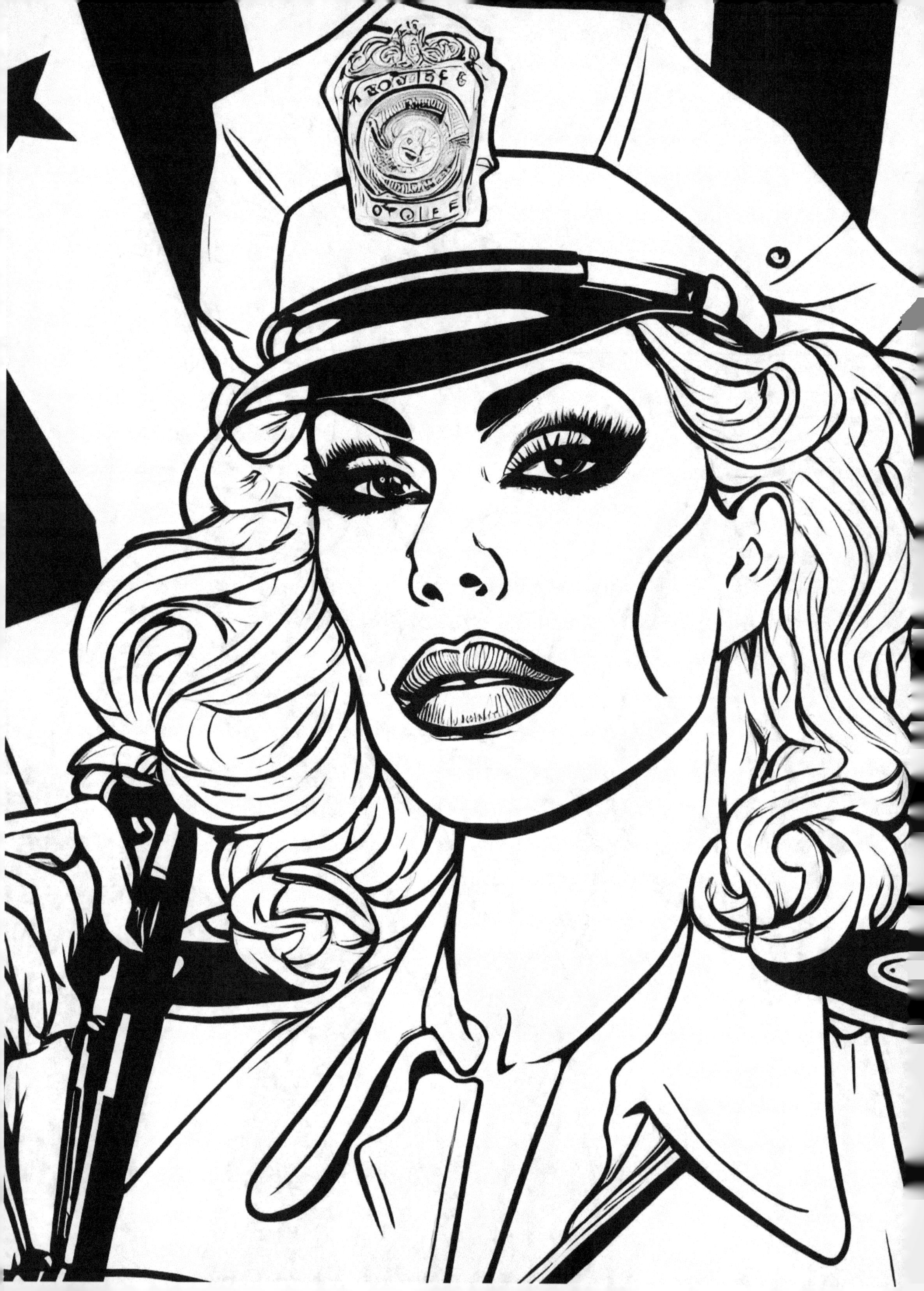

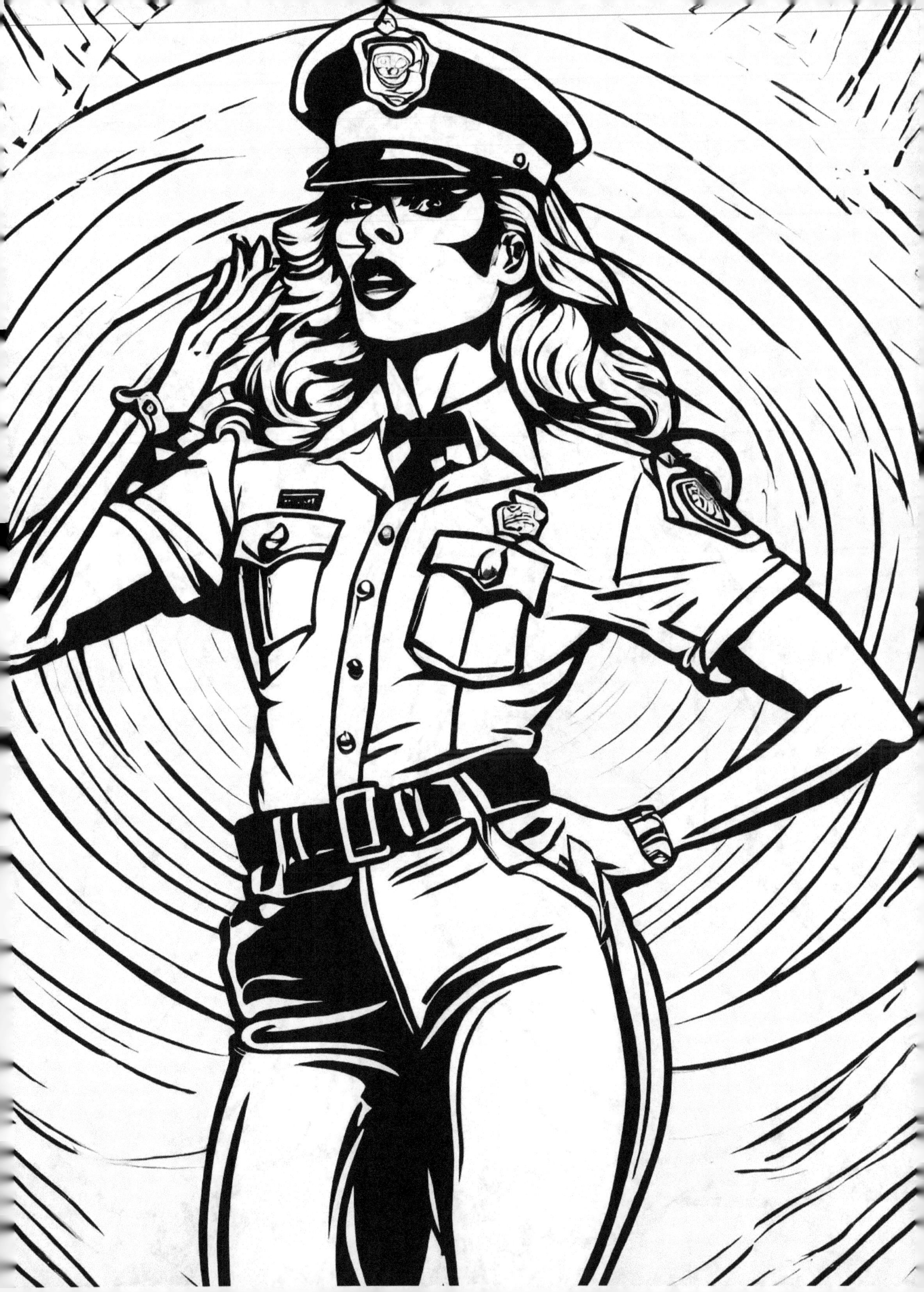

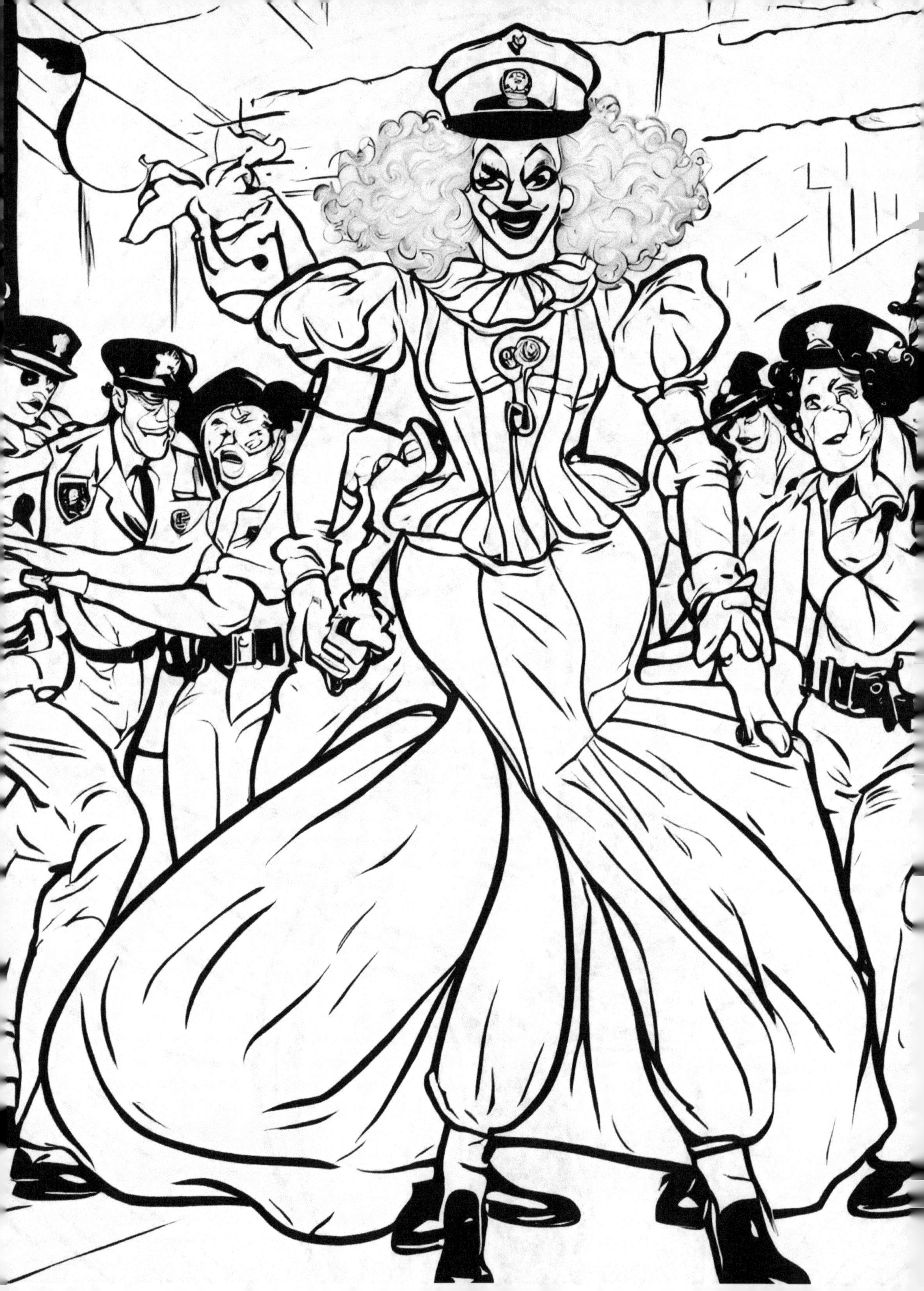

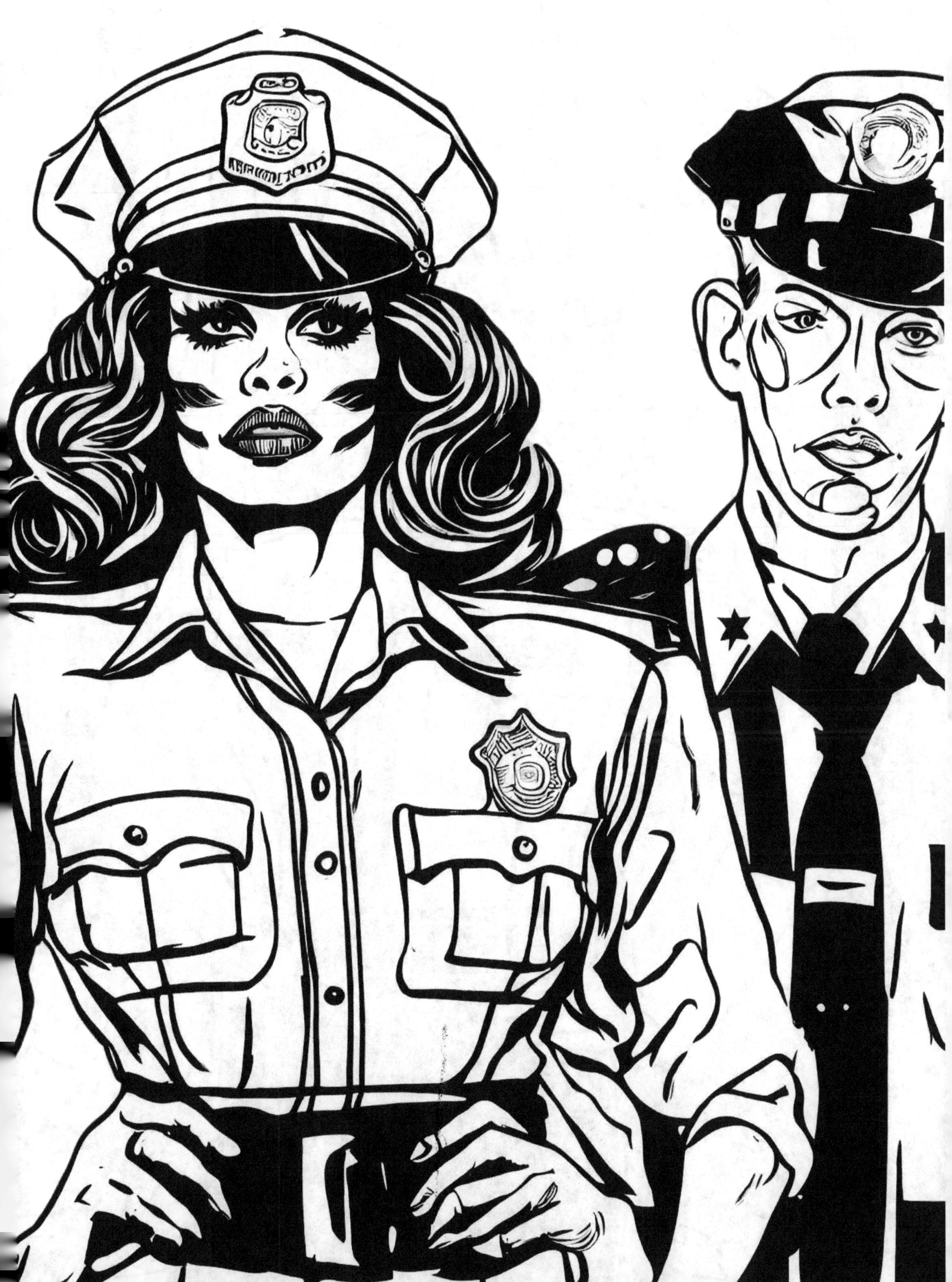

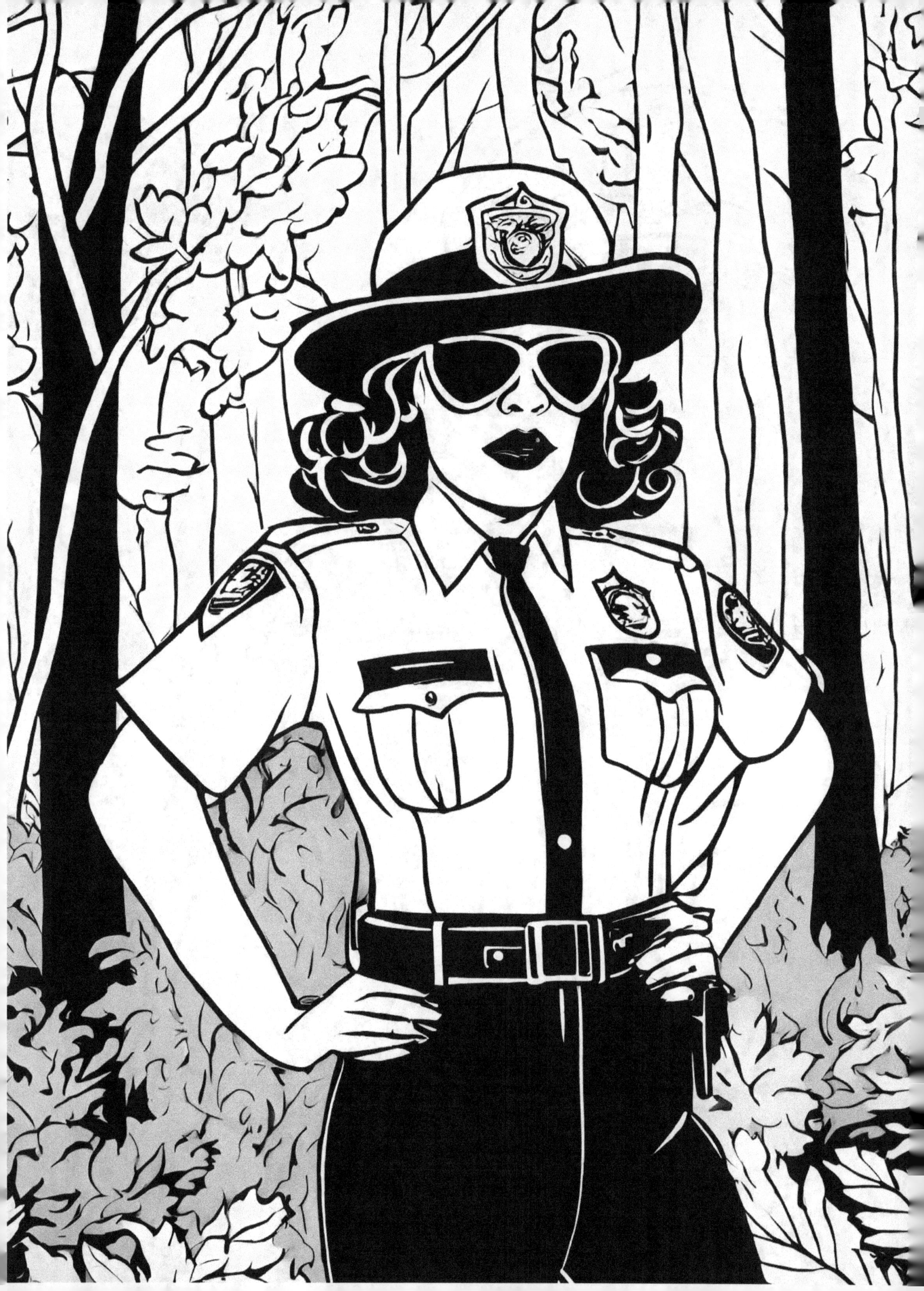

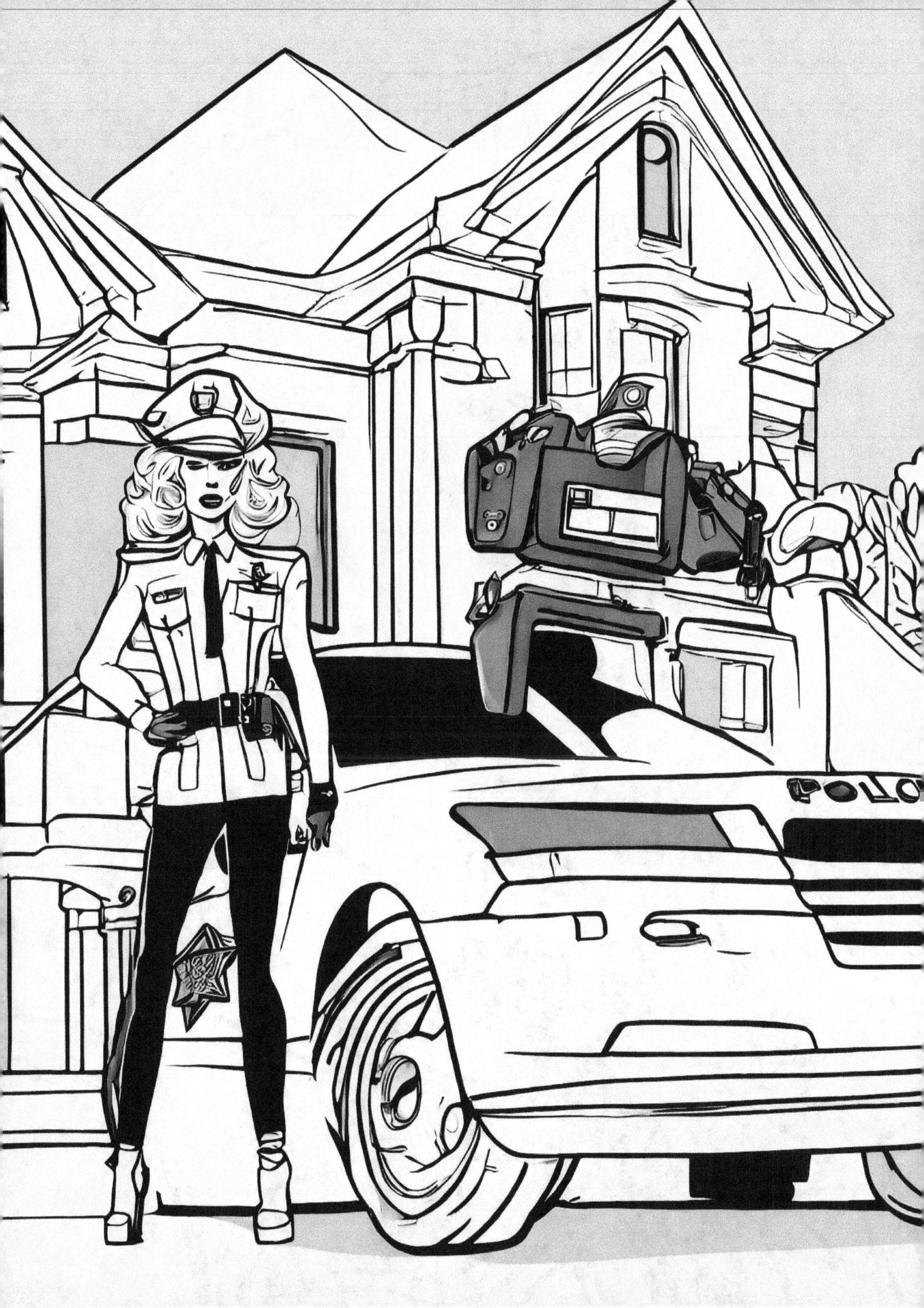
POLO

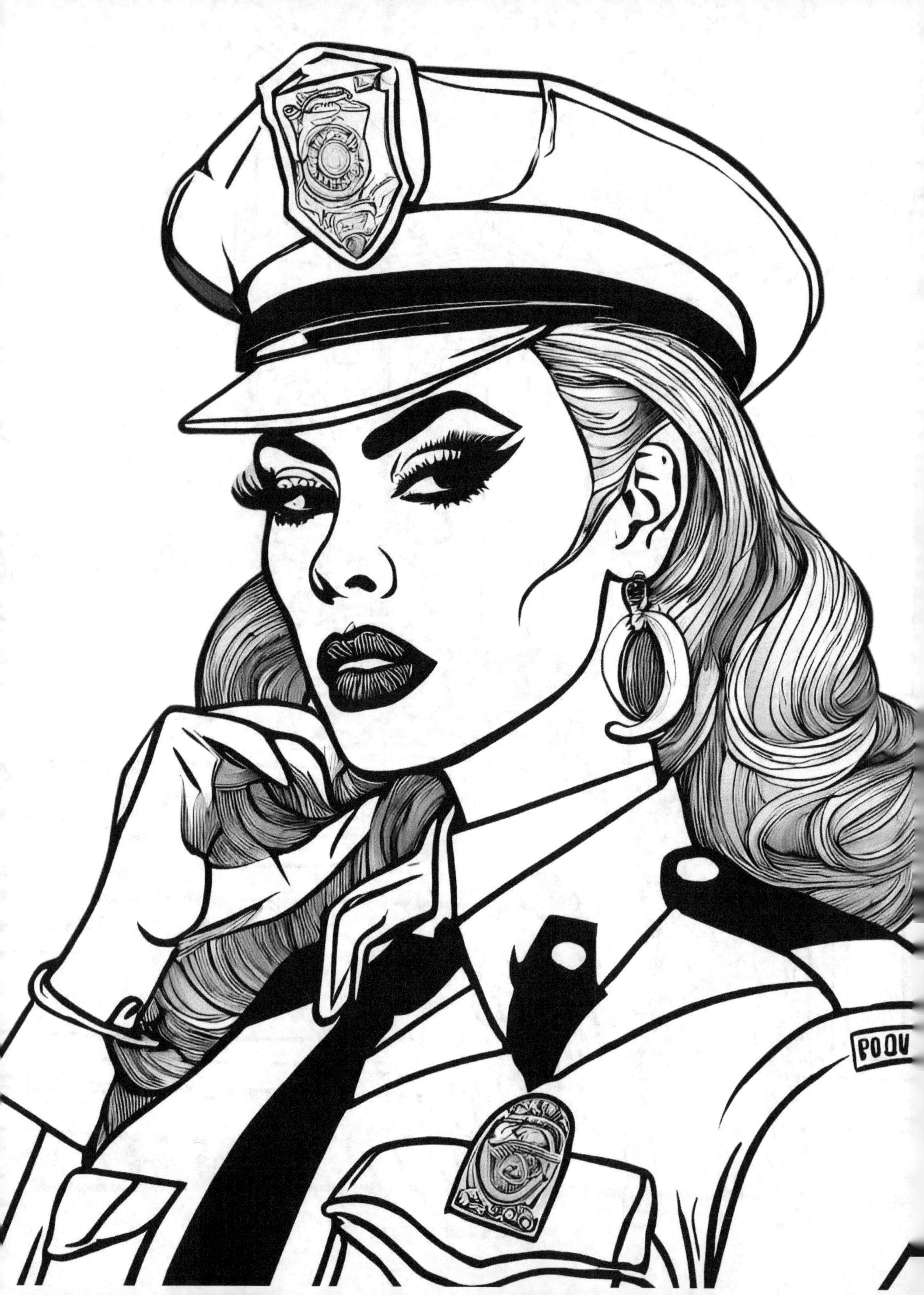
POQV

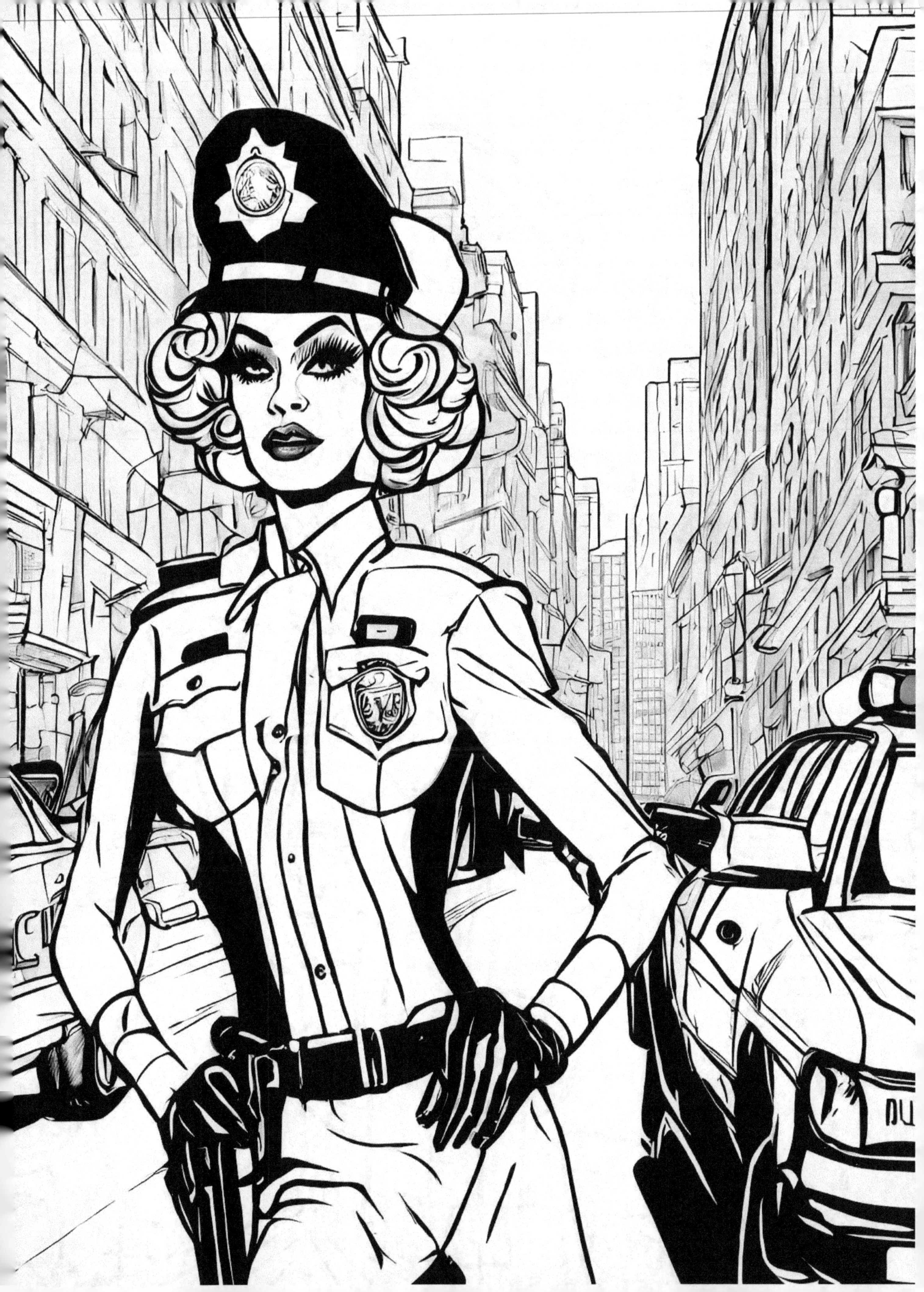

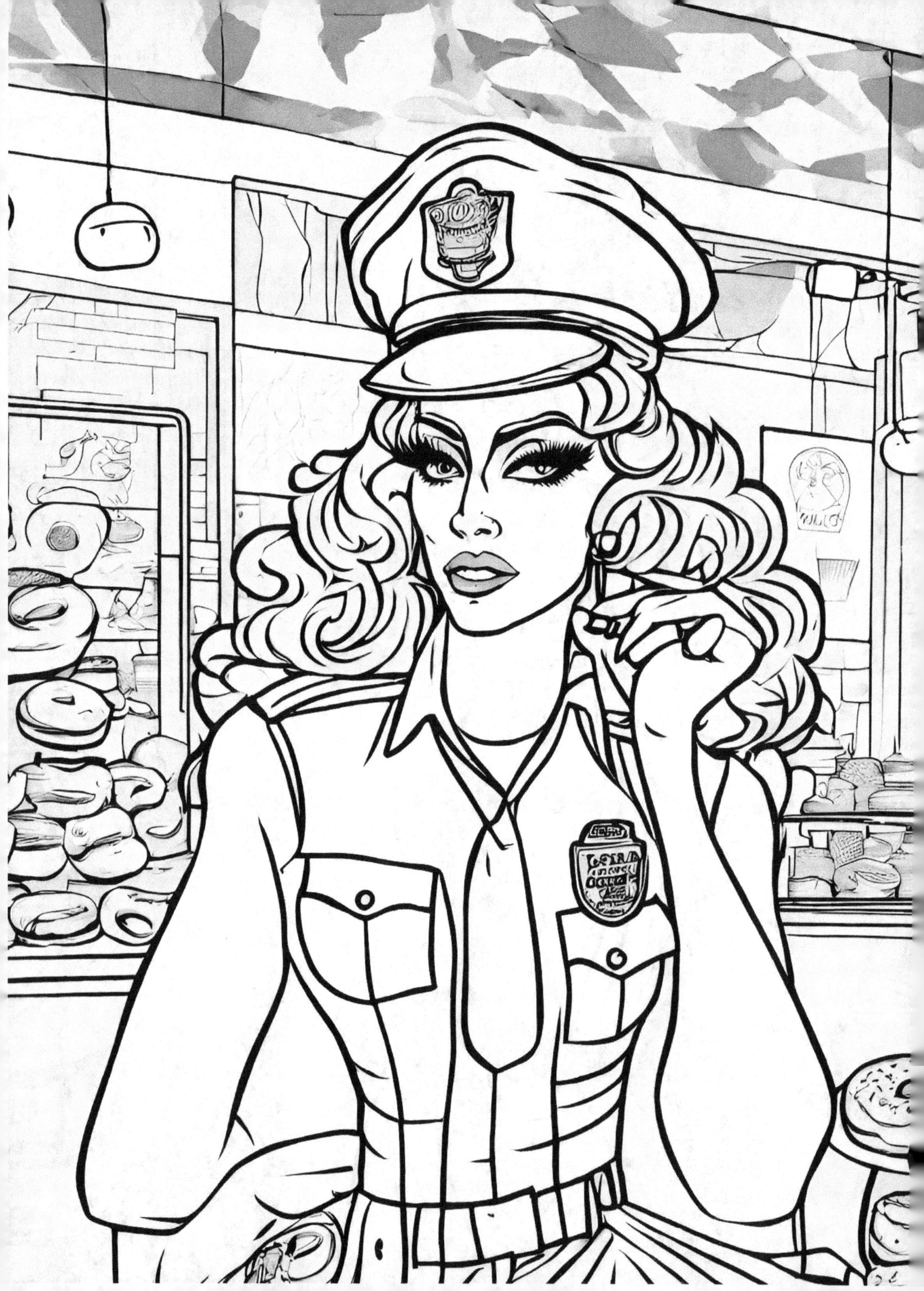

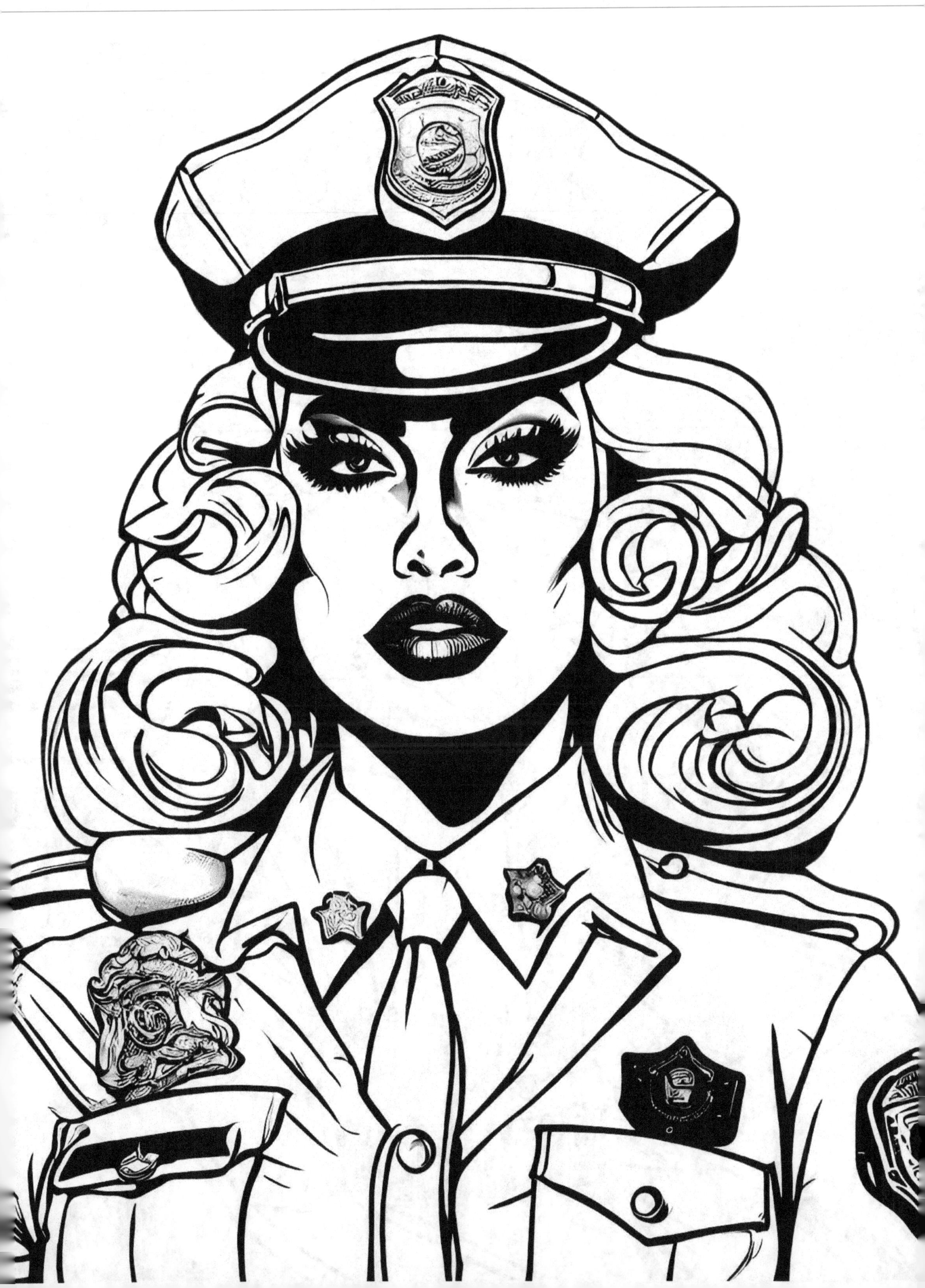

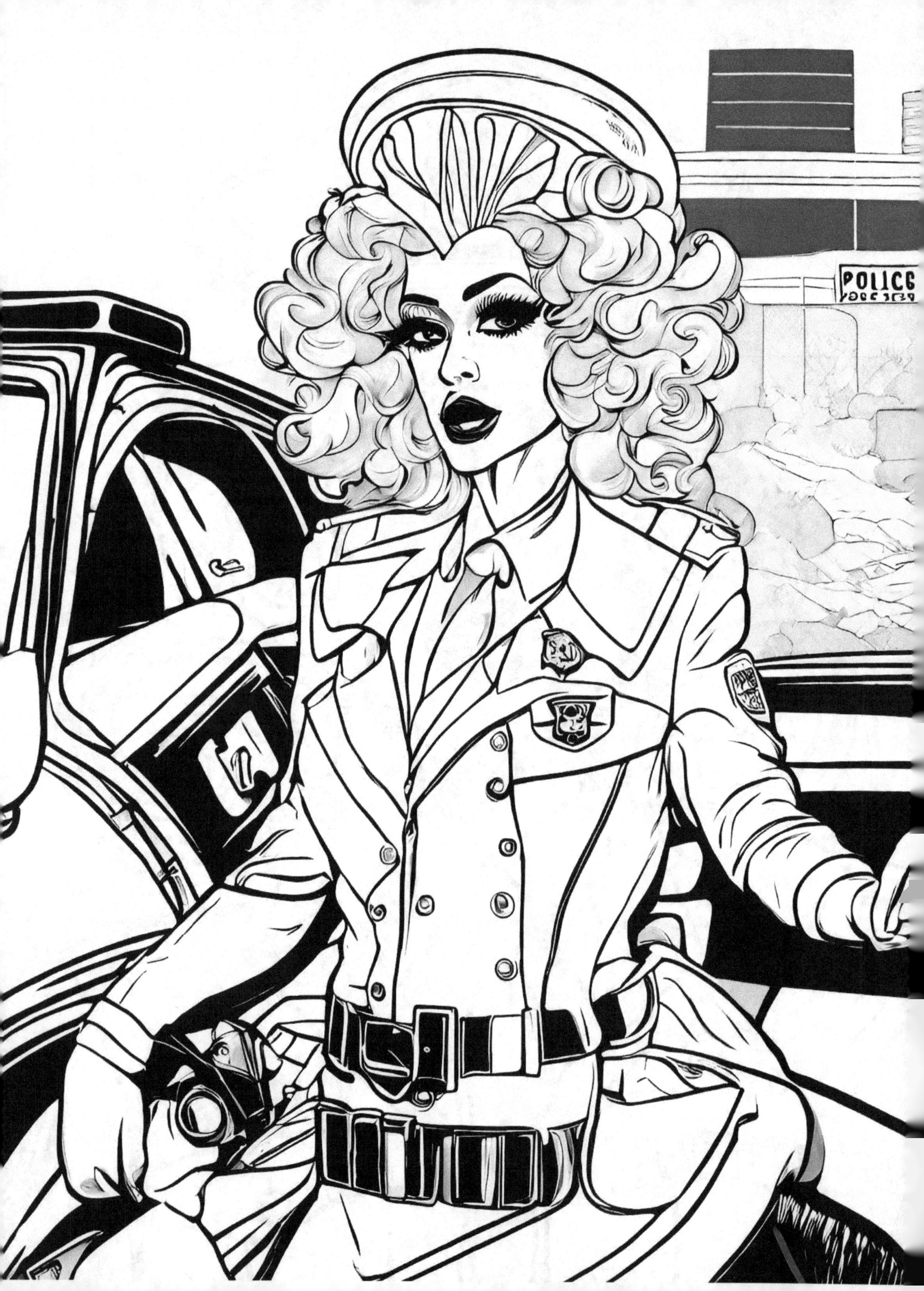

POLICE

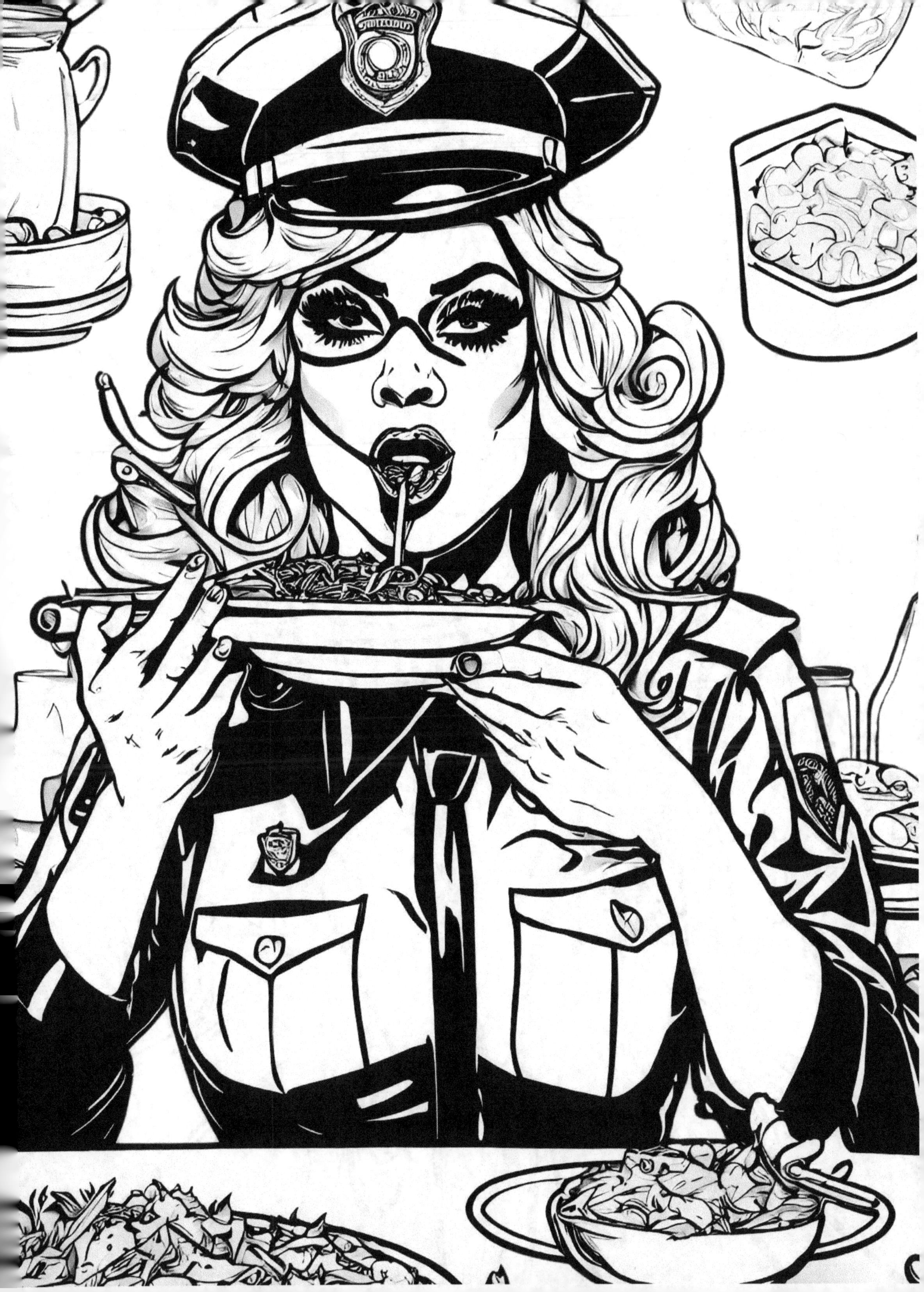

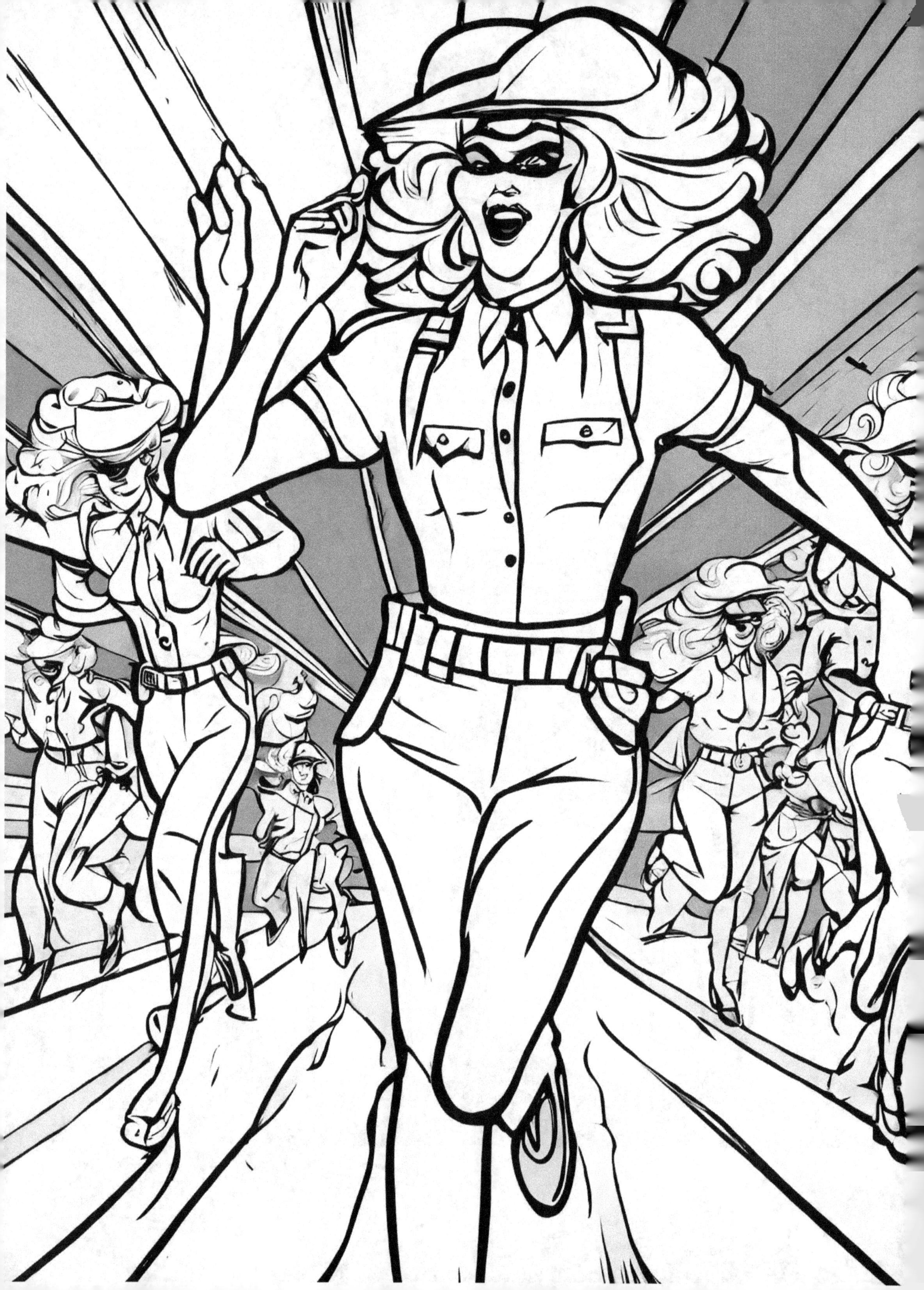

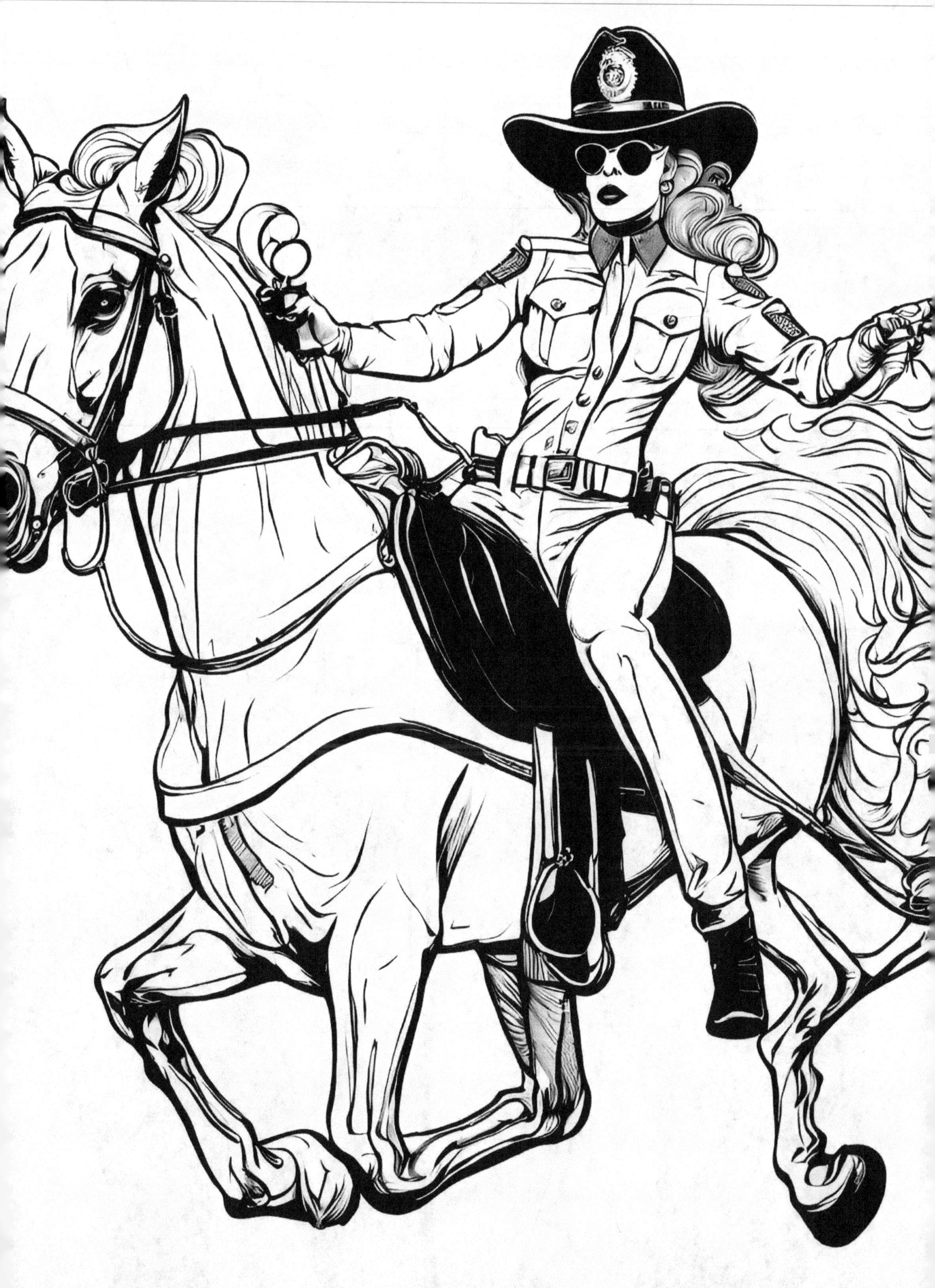

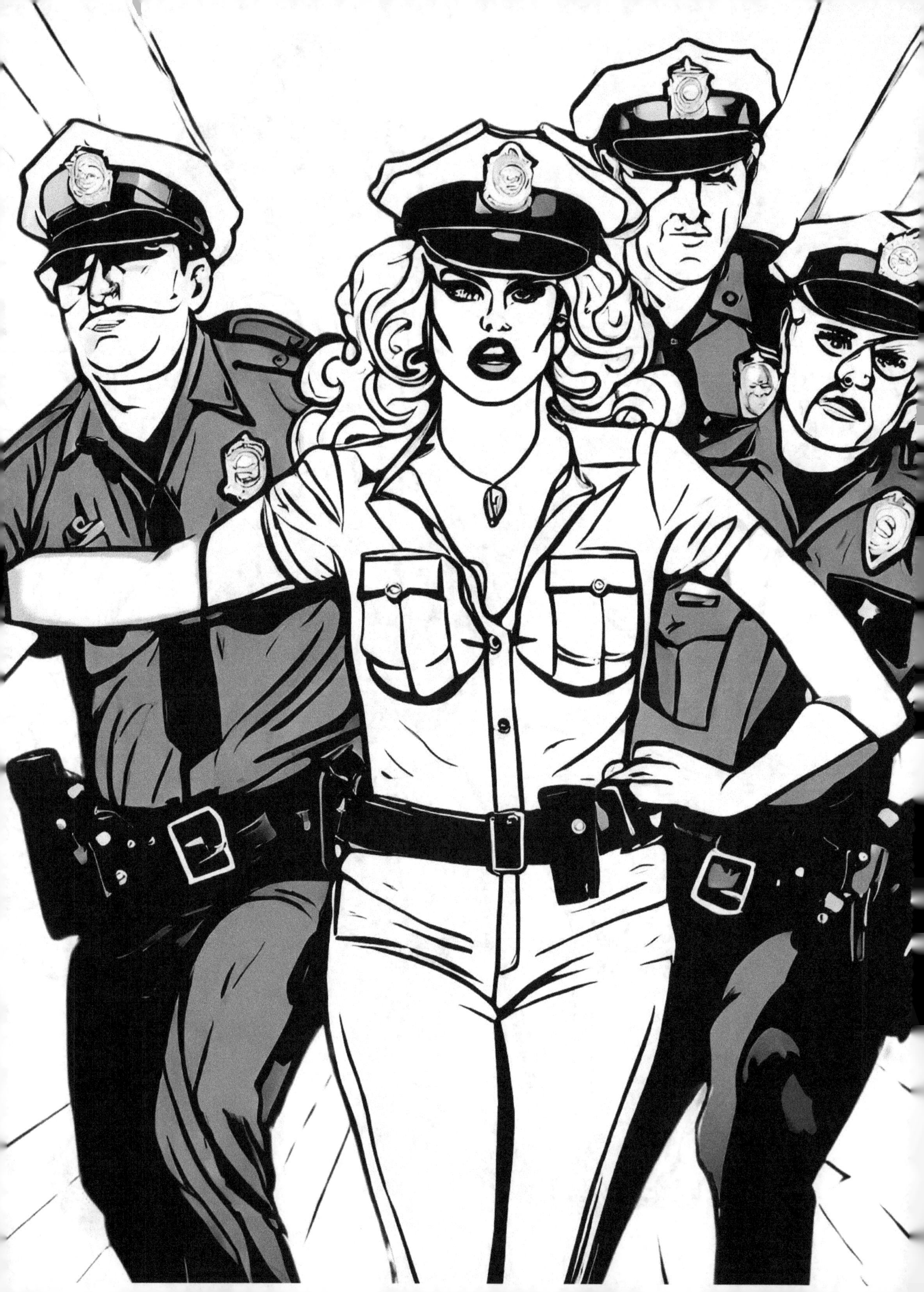

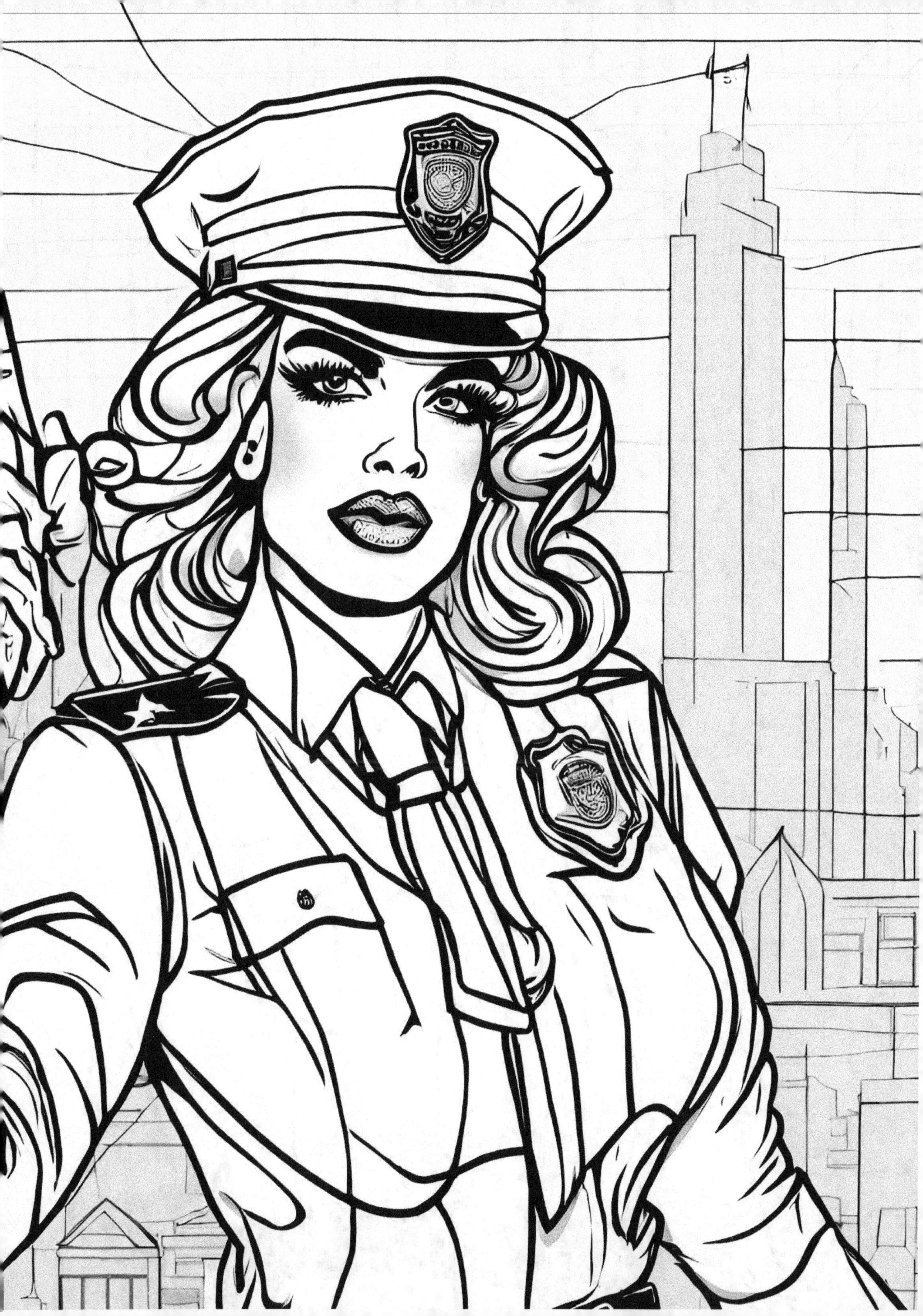

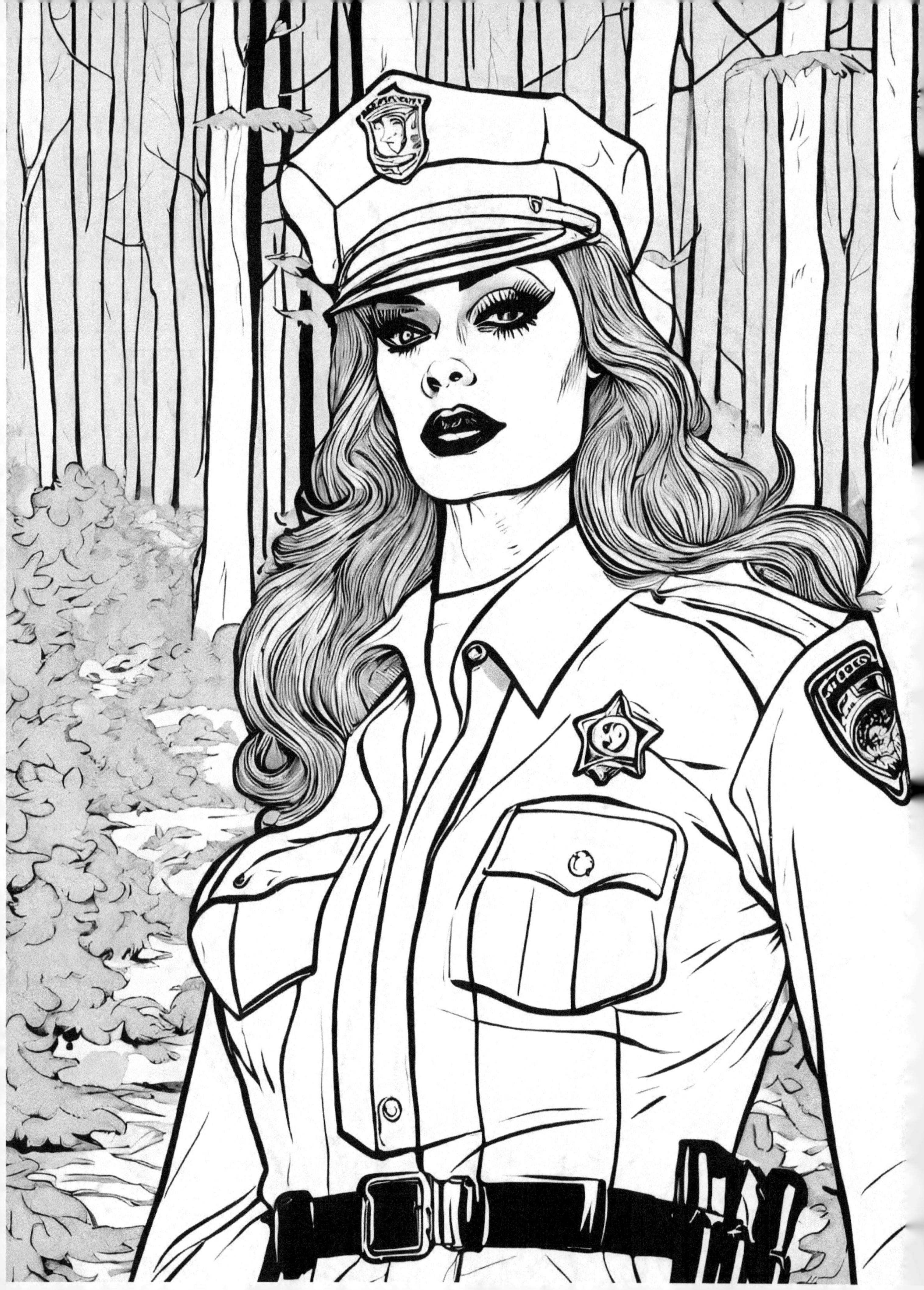

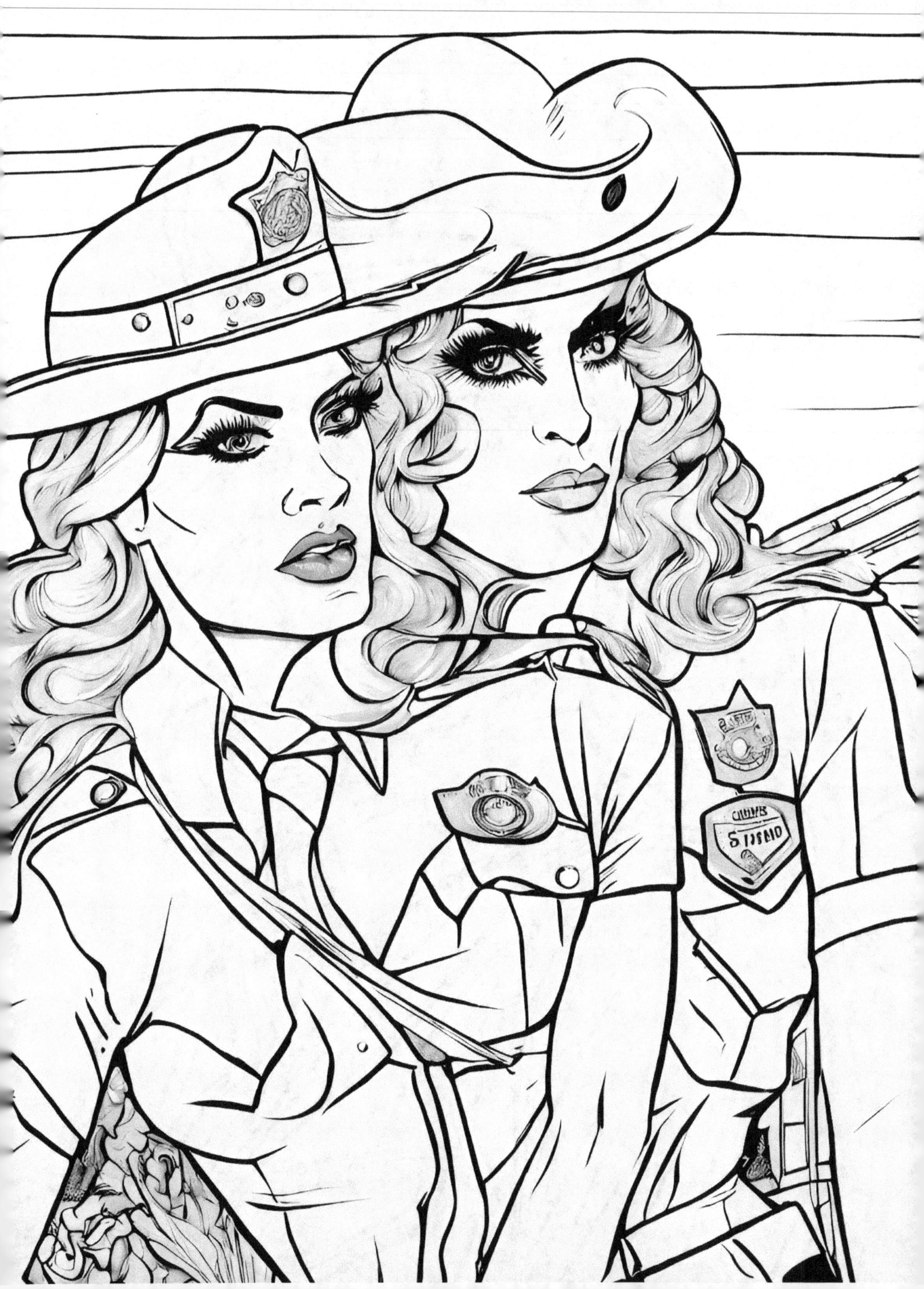

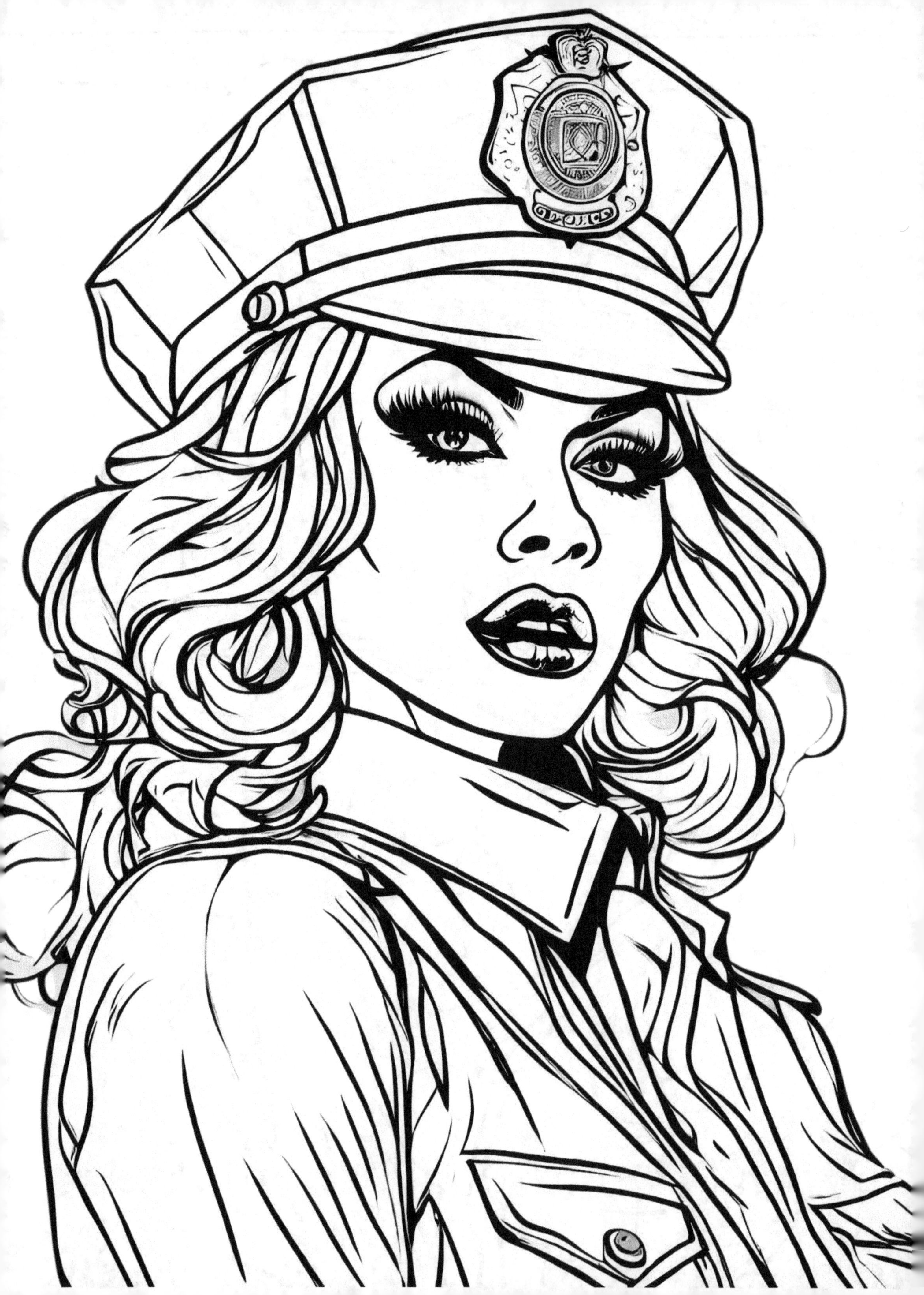

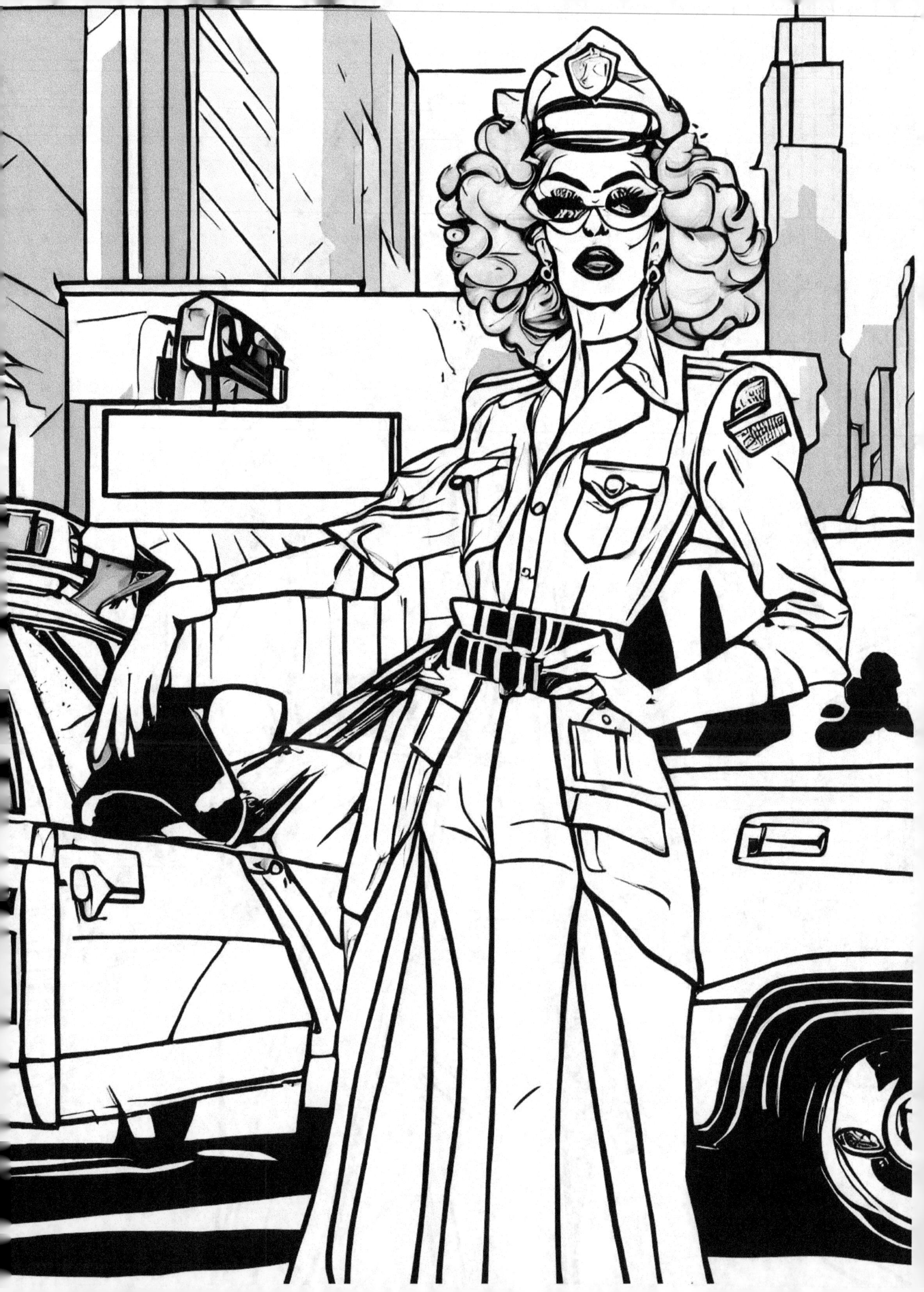

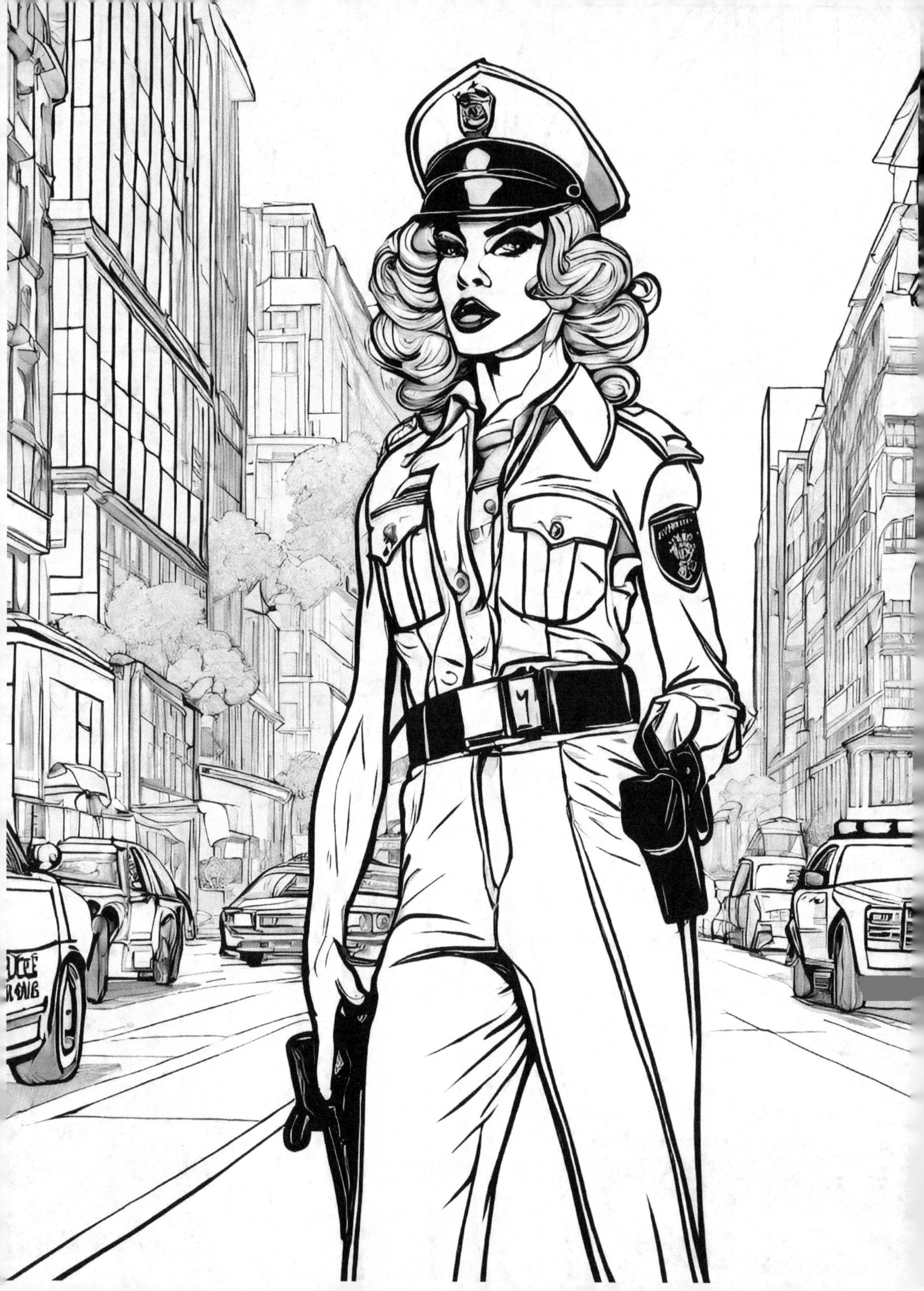

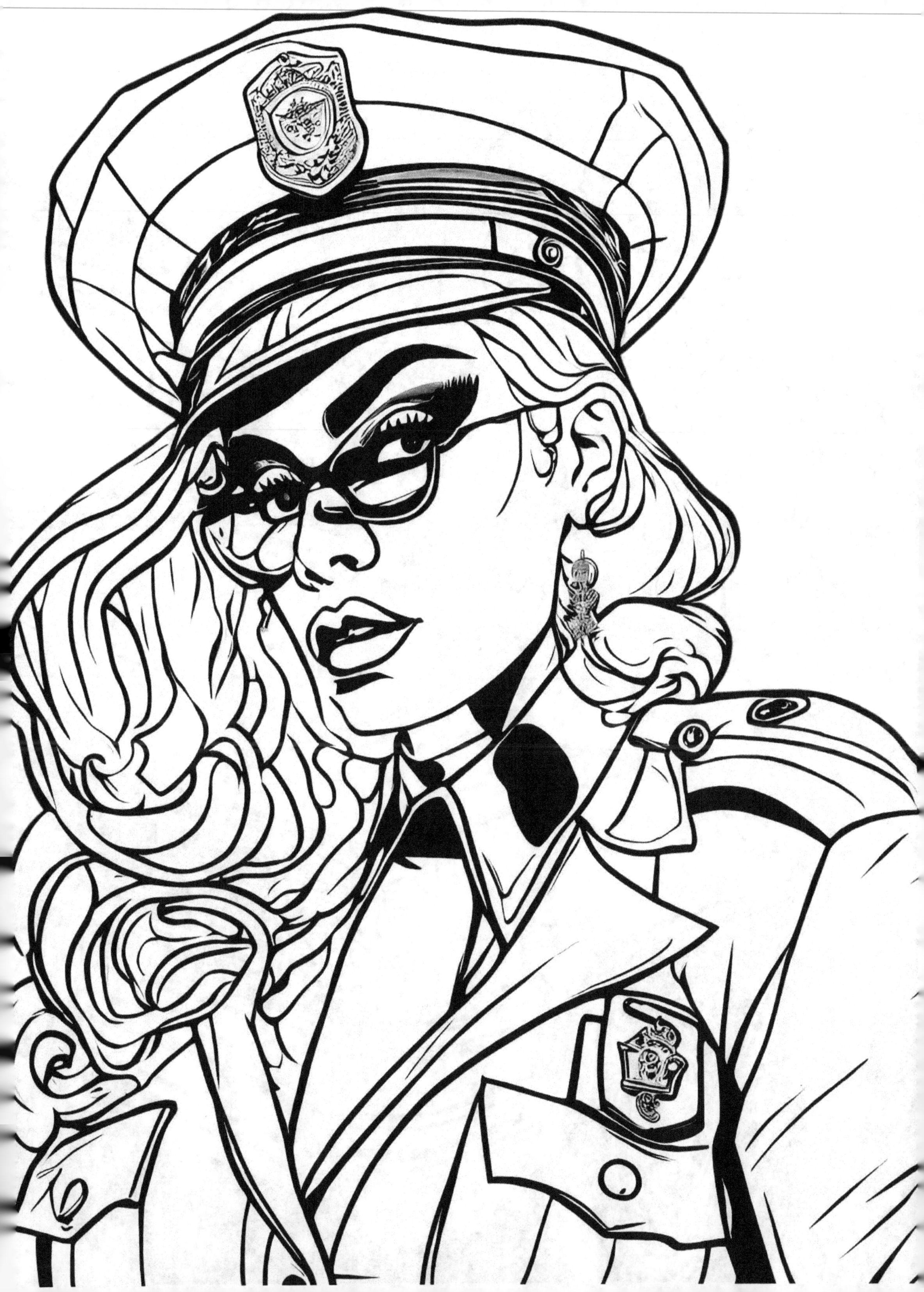

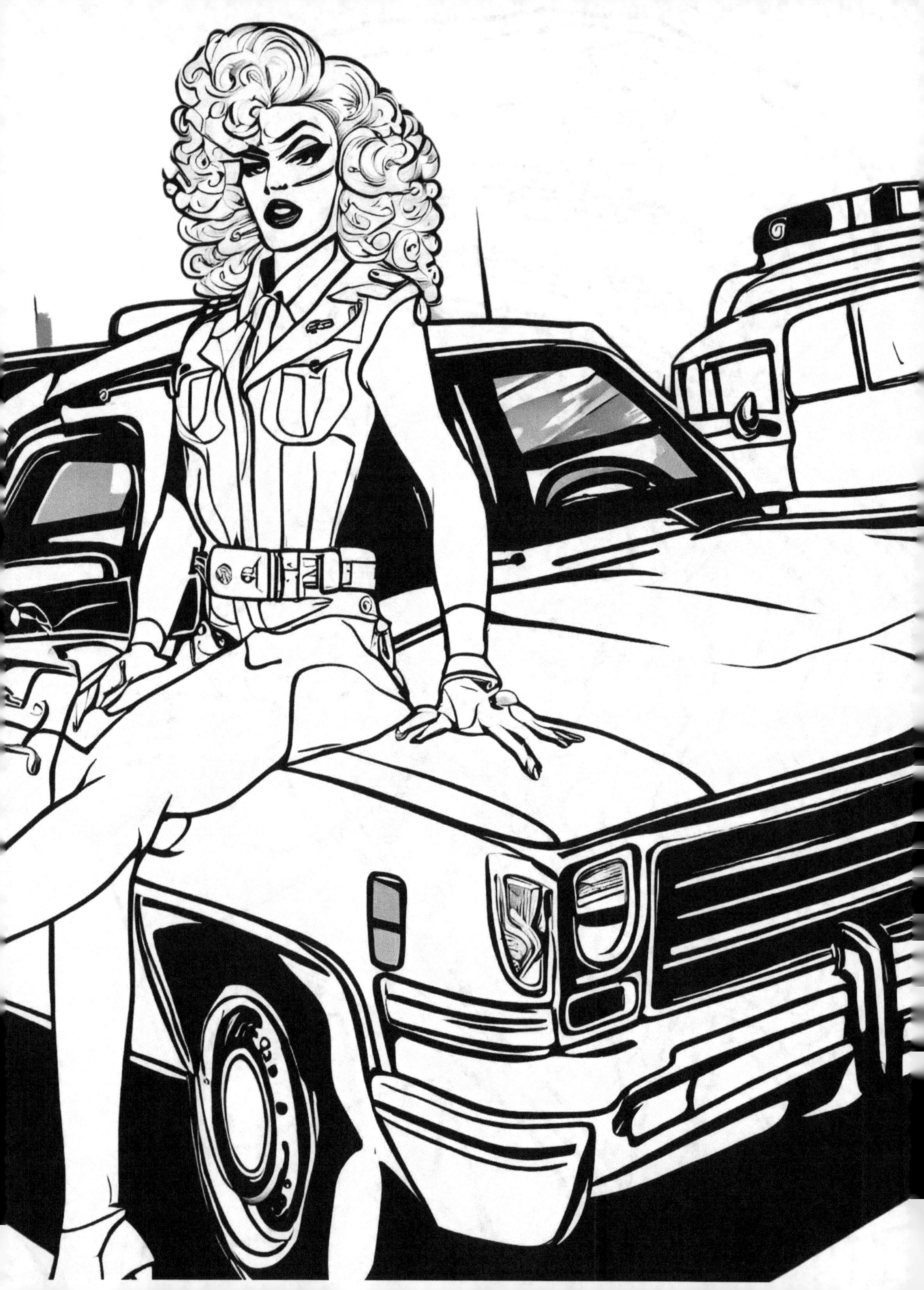

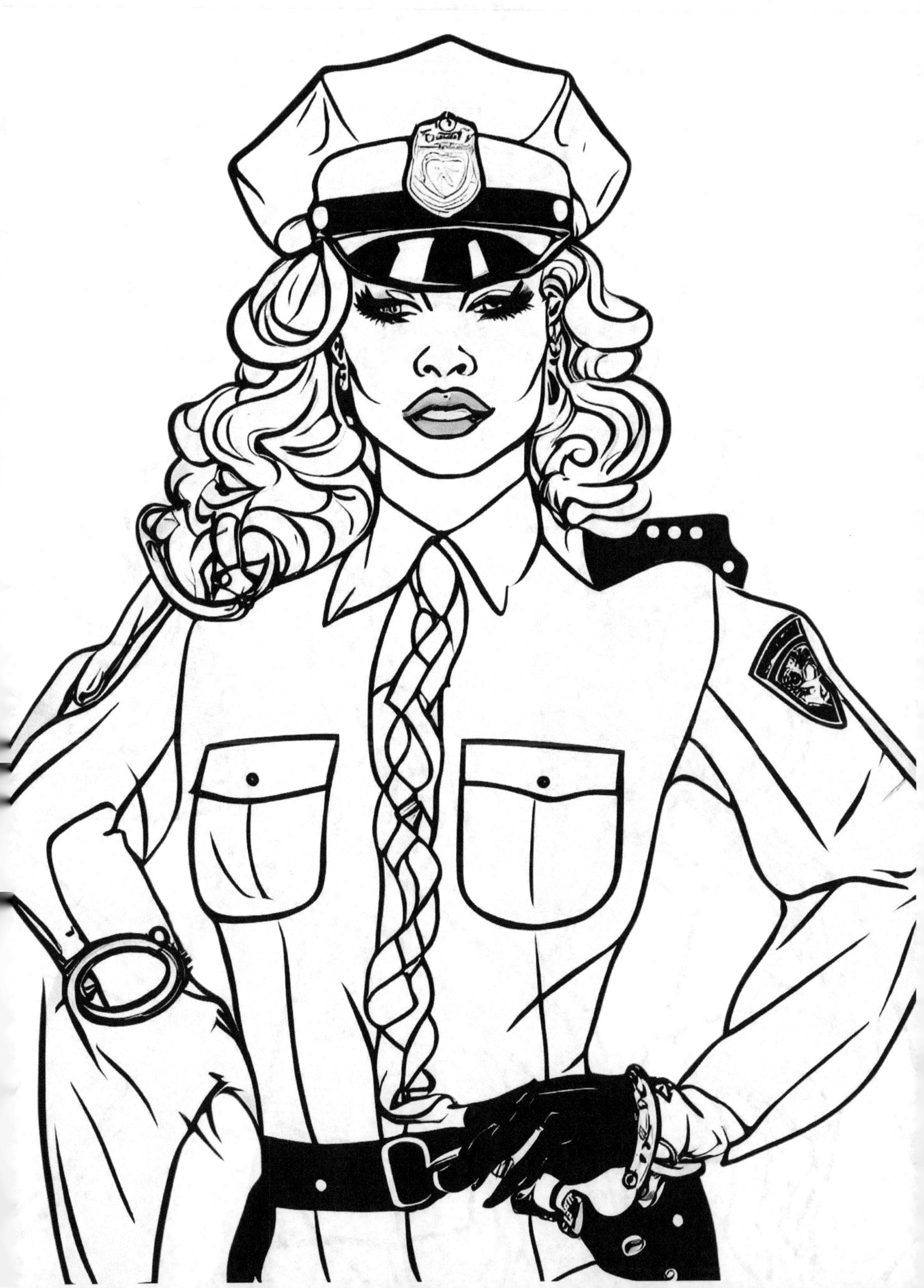

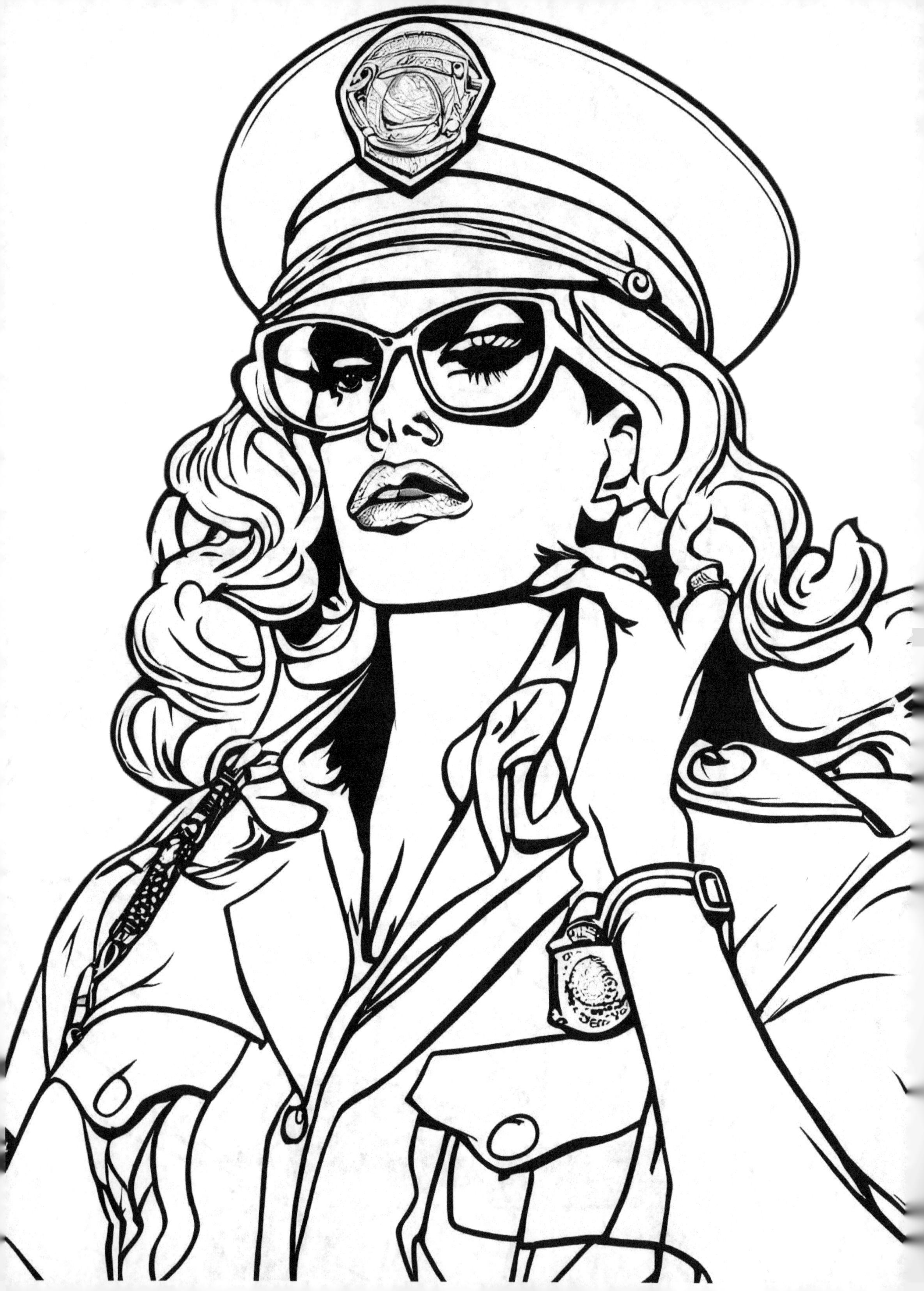

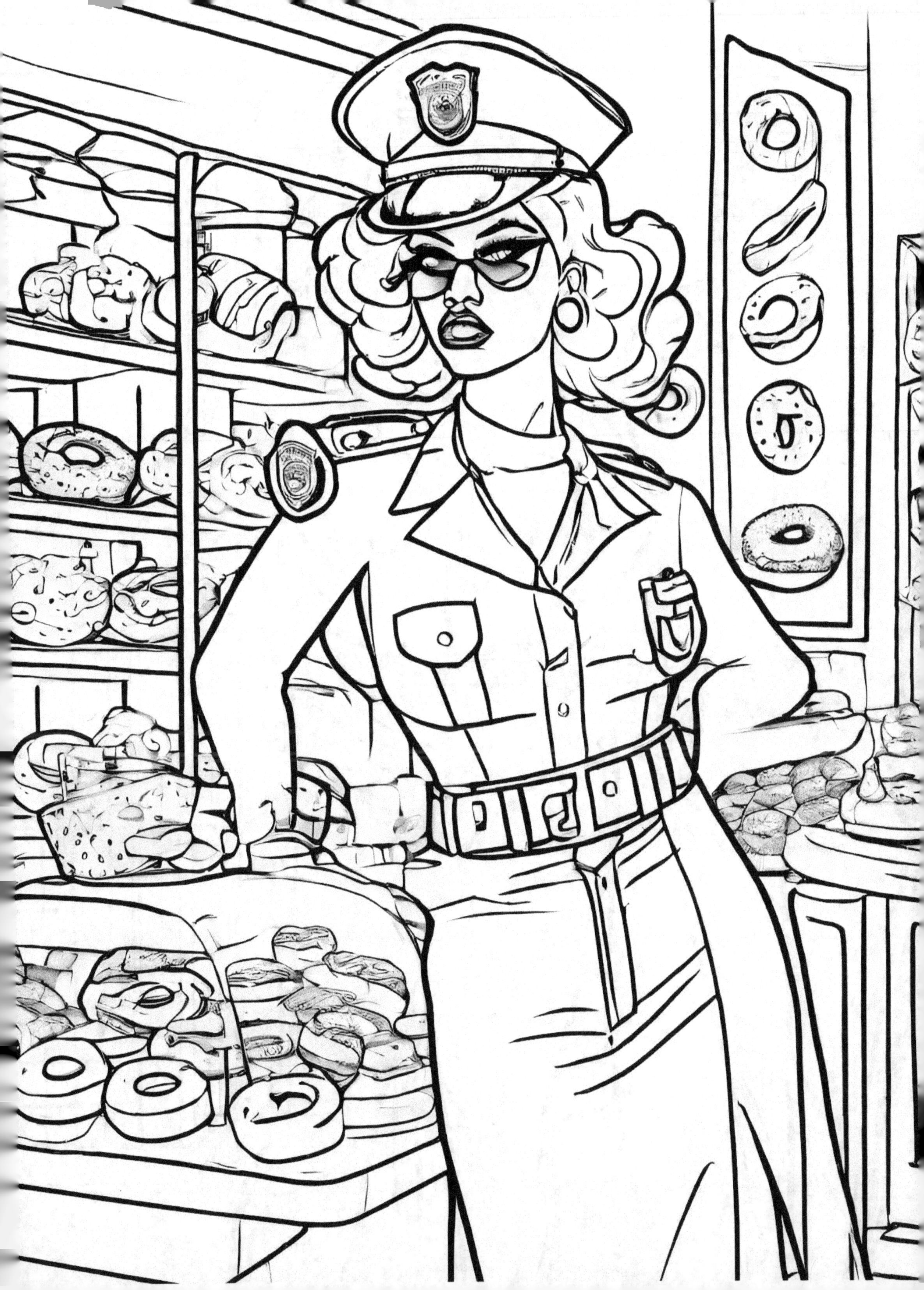

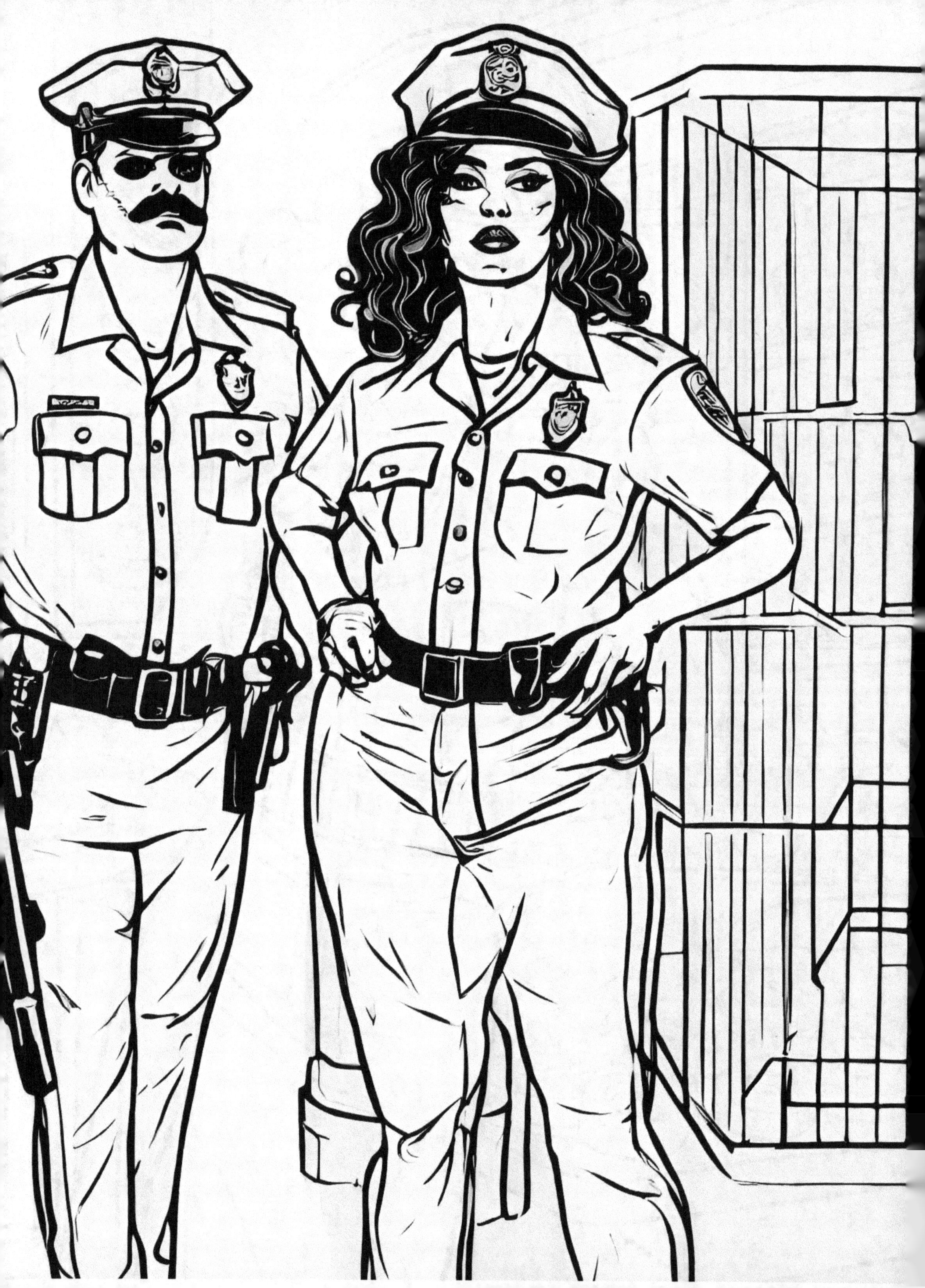

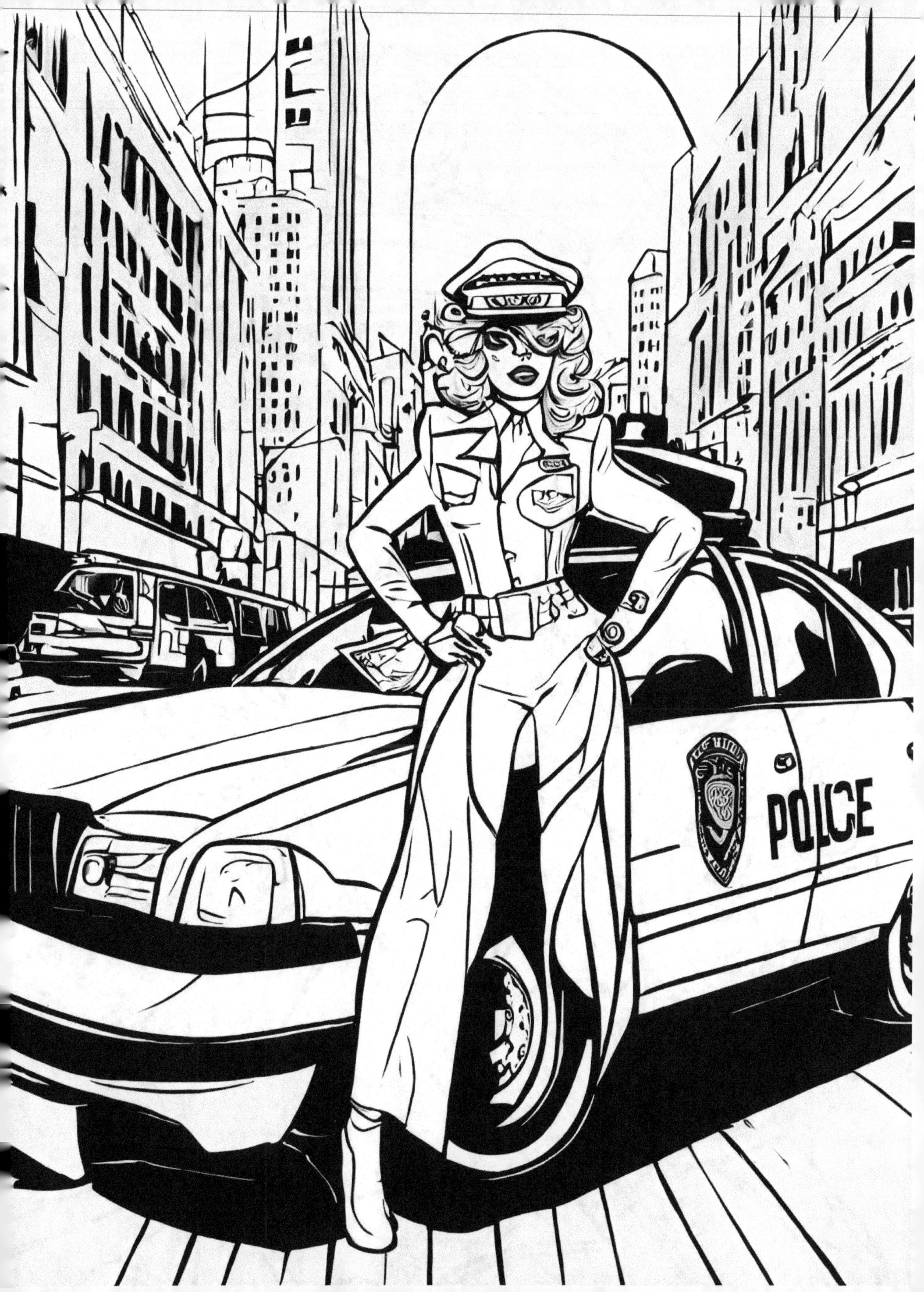
POLICE

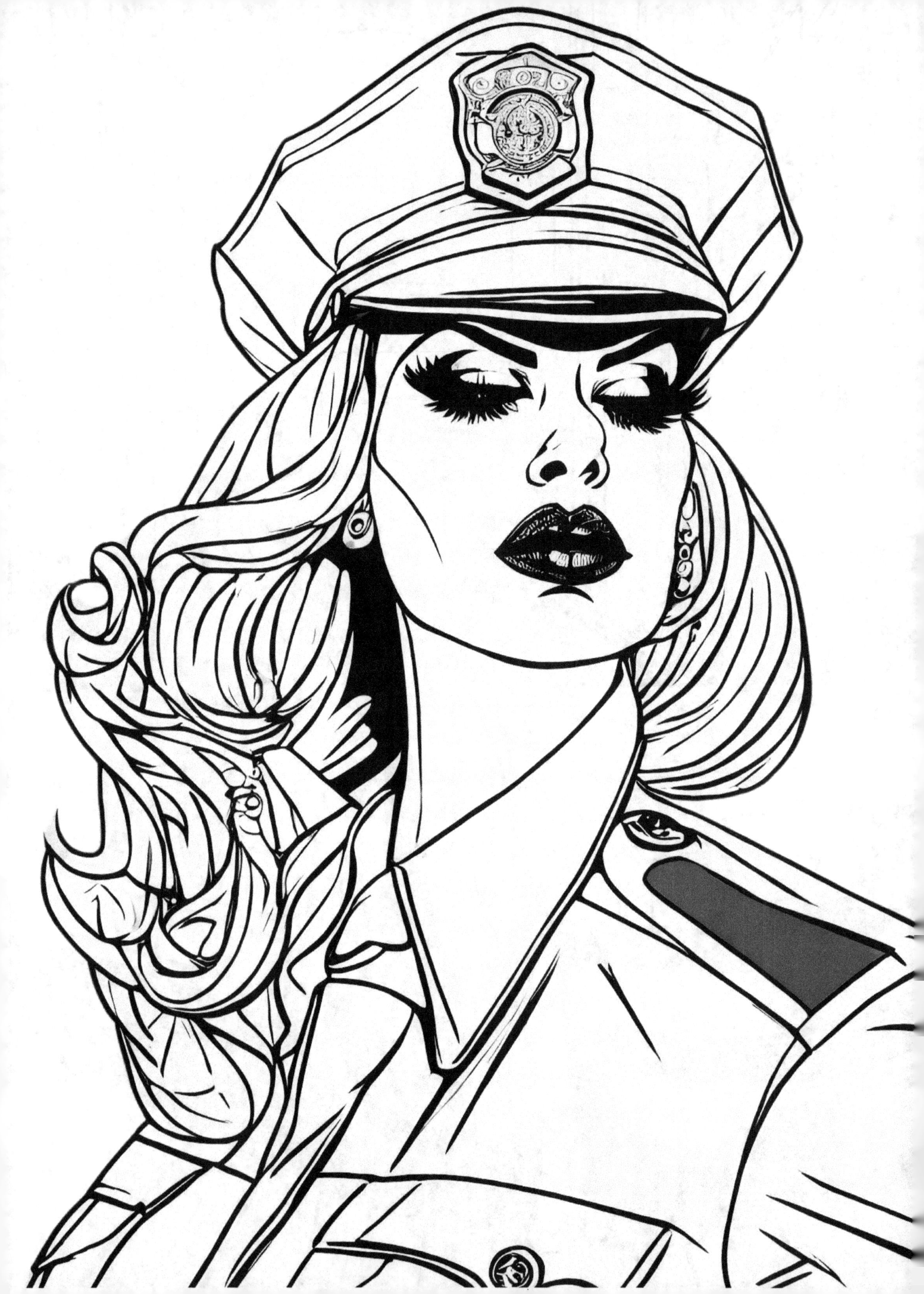

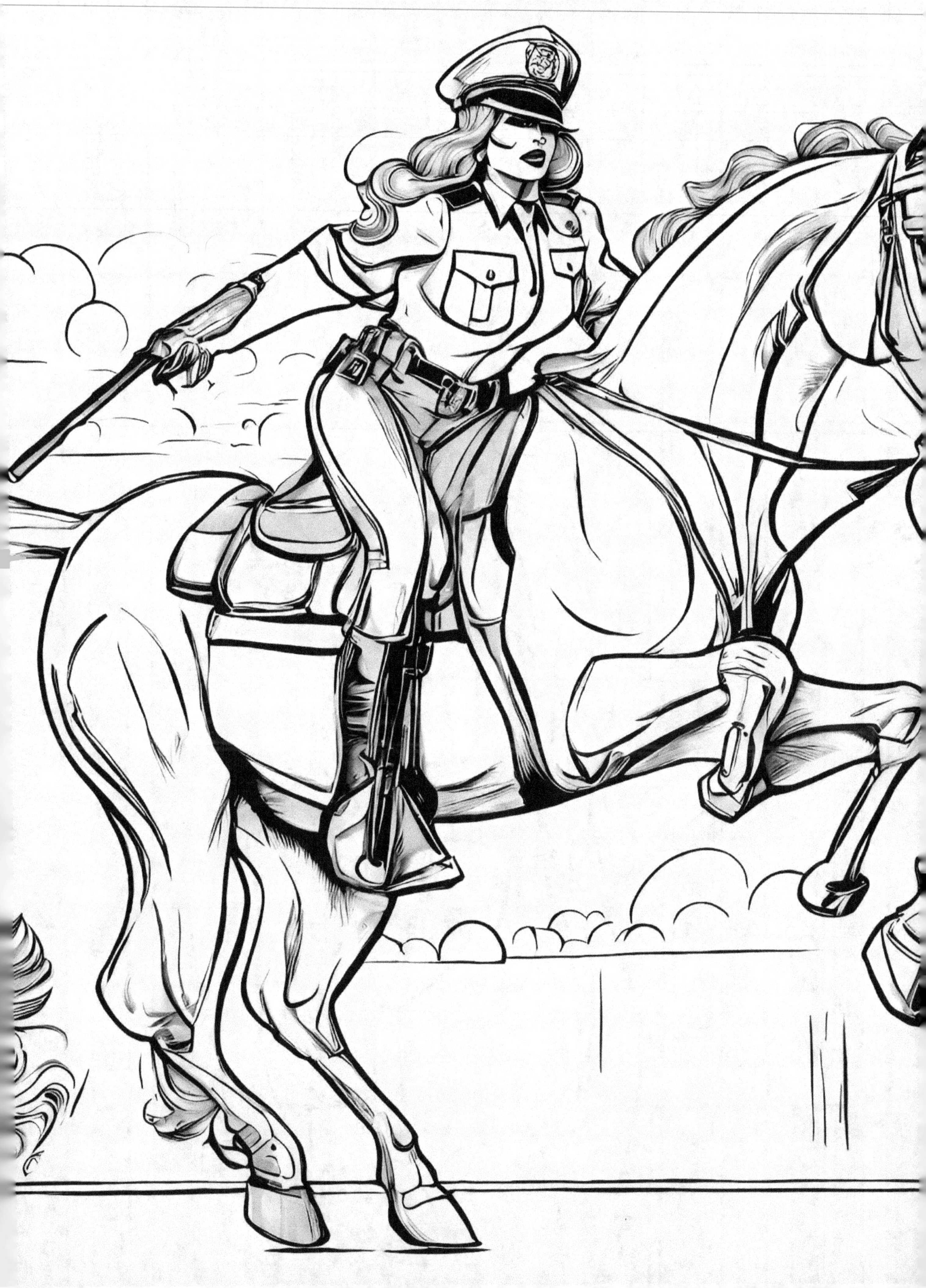

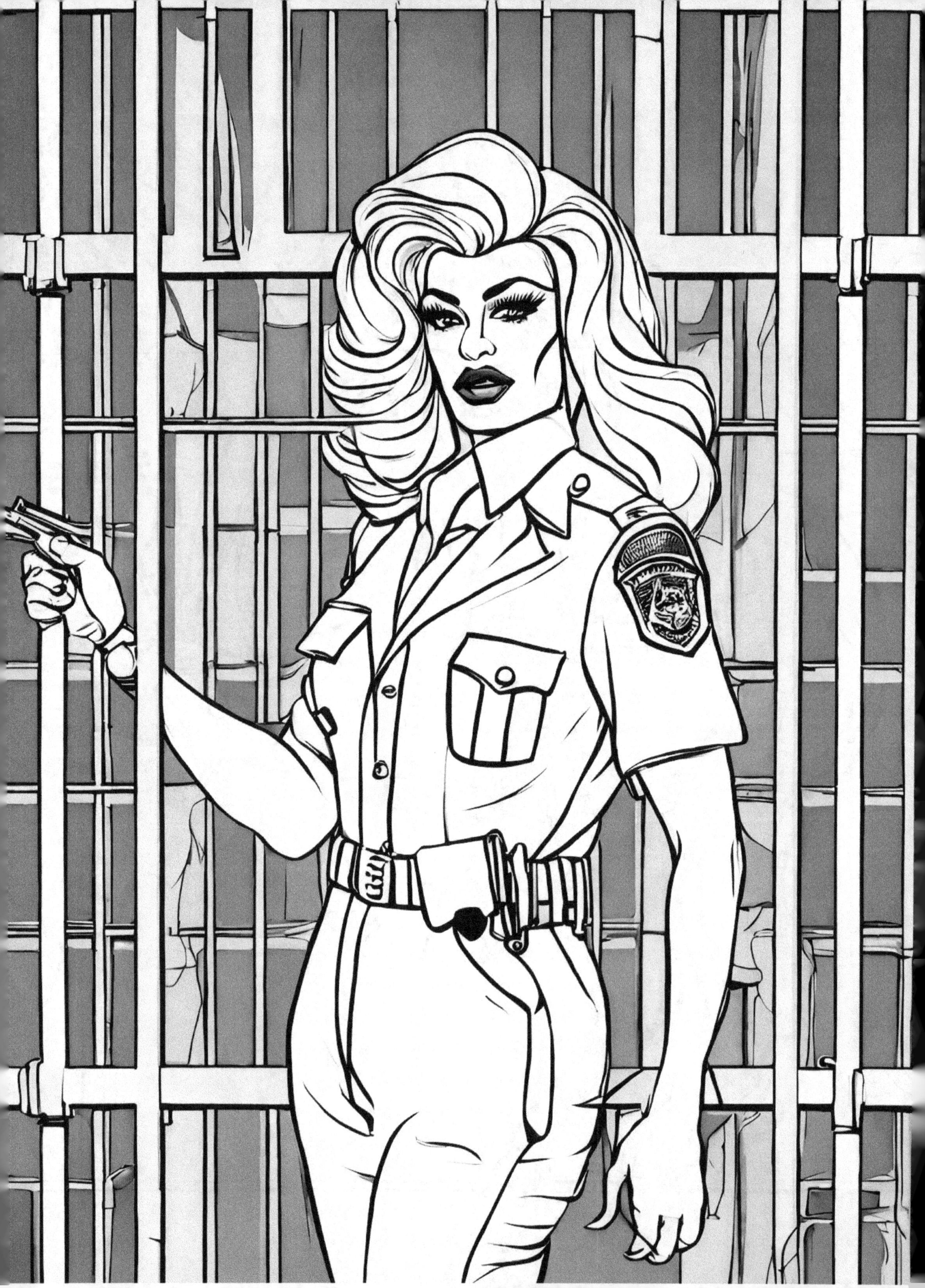

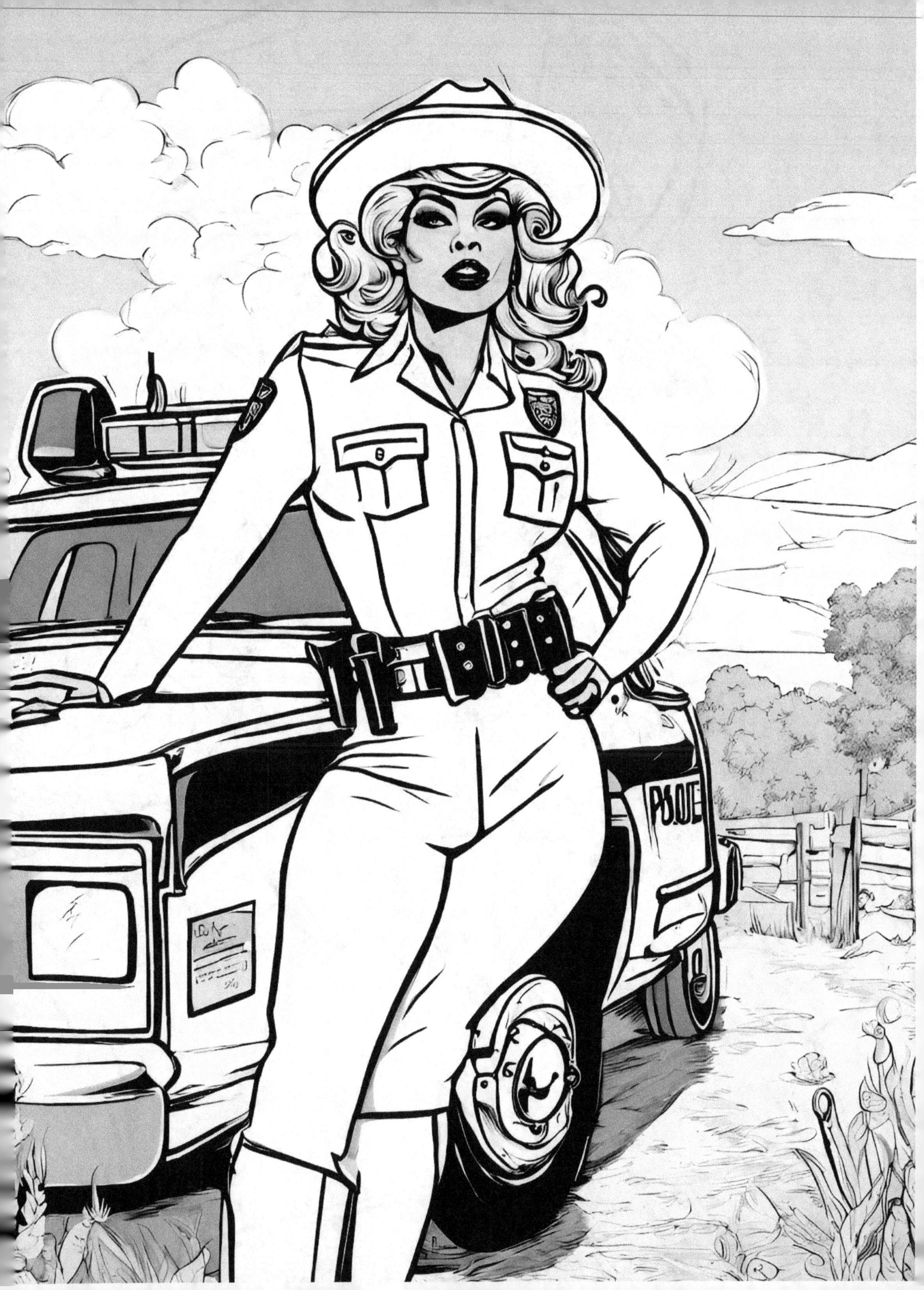

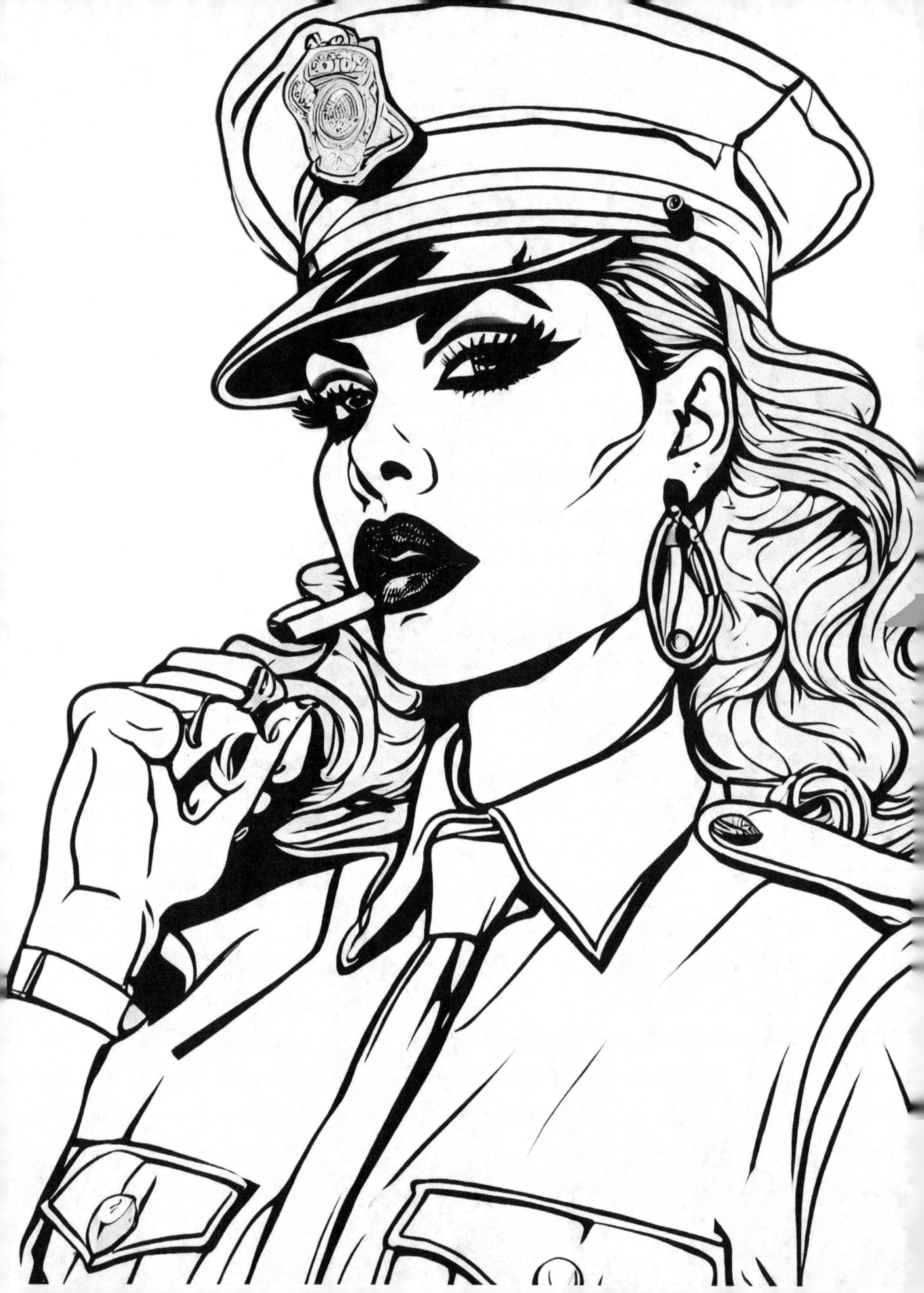

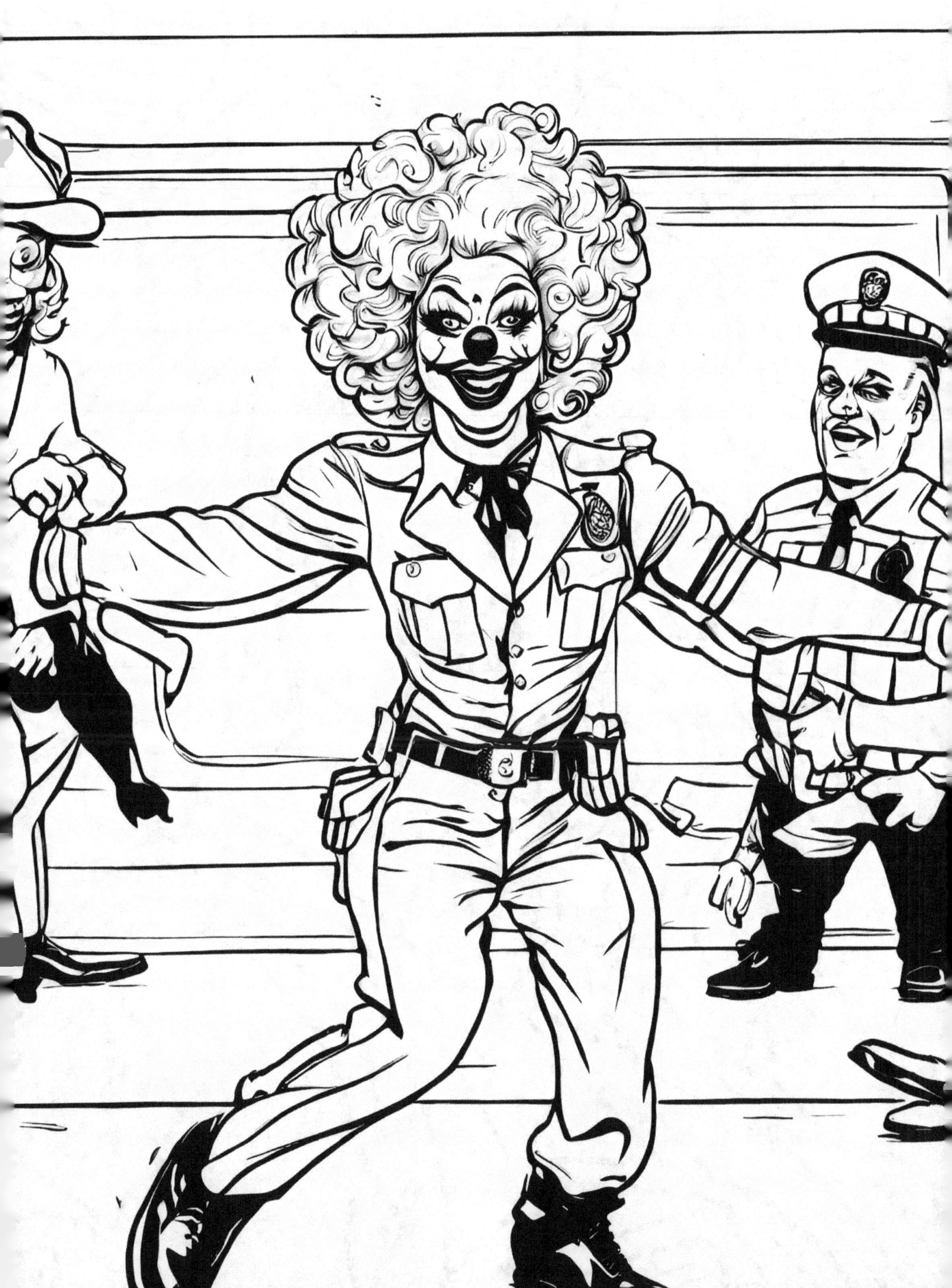

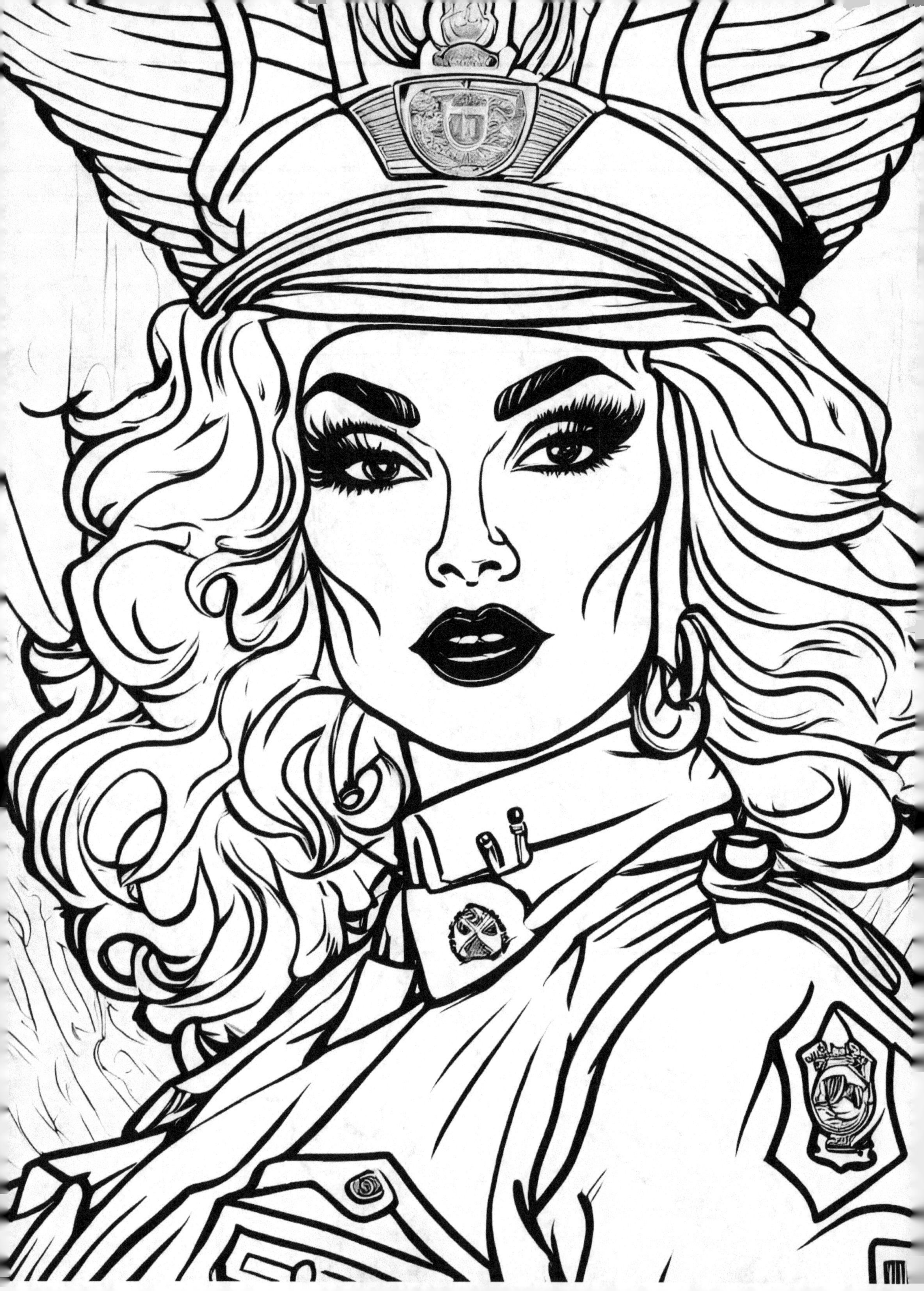

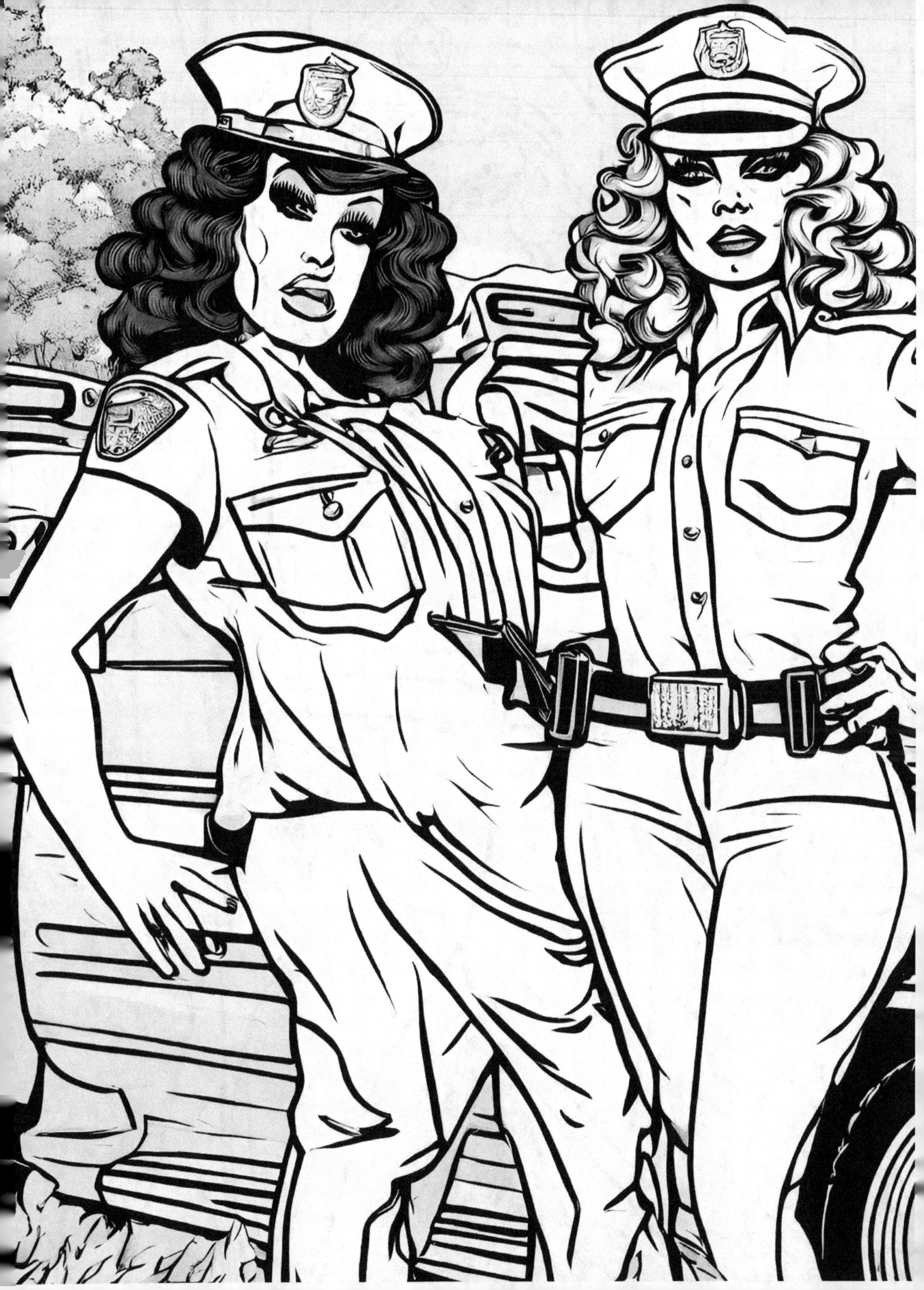

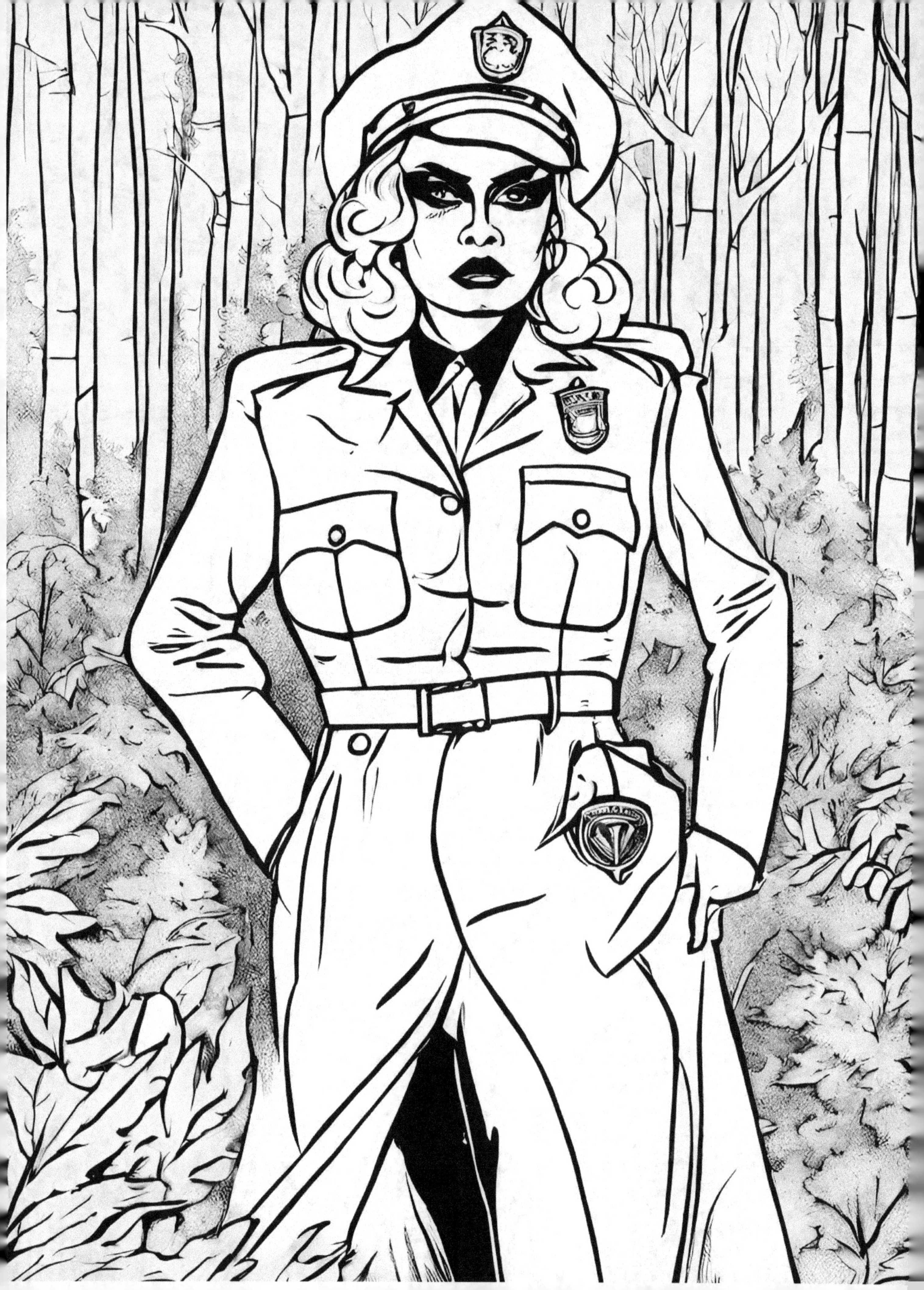

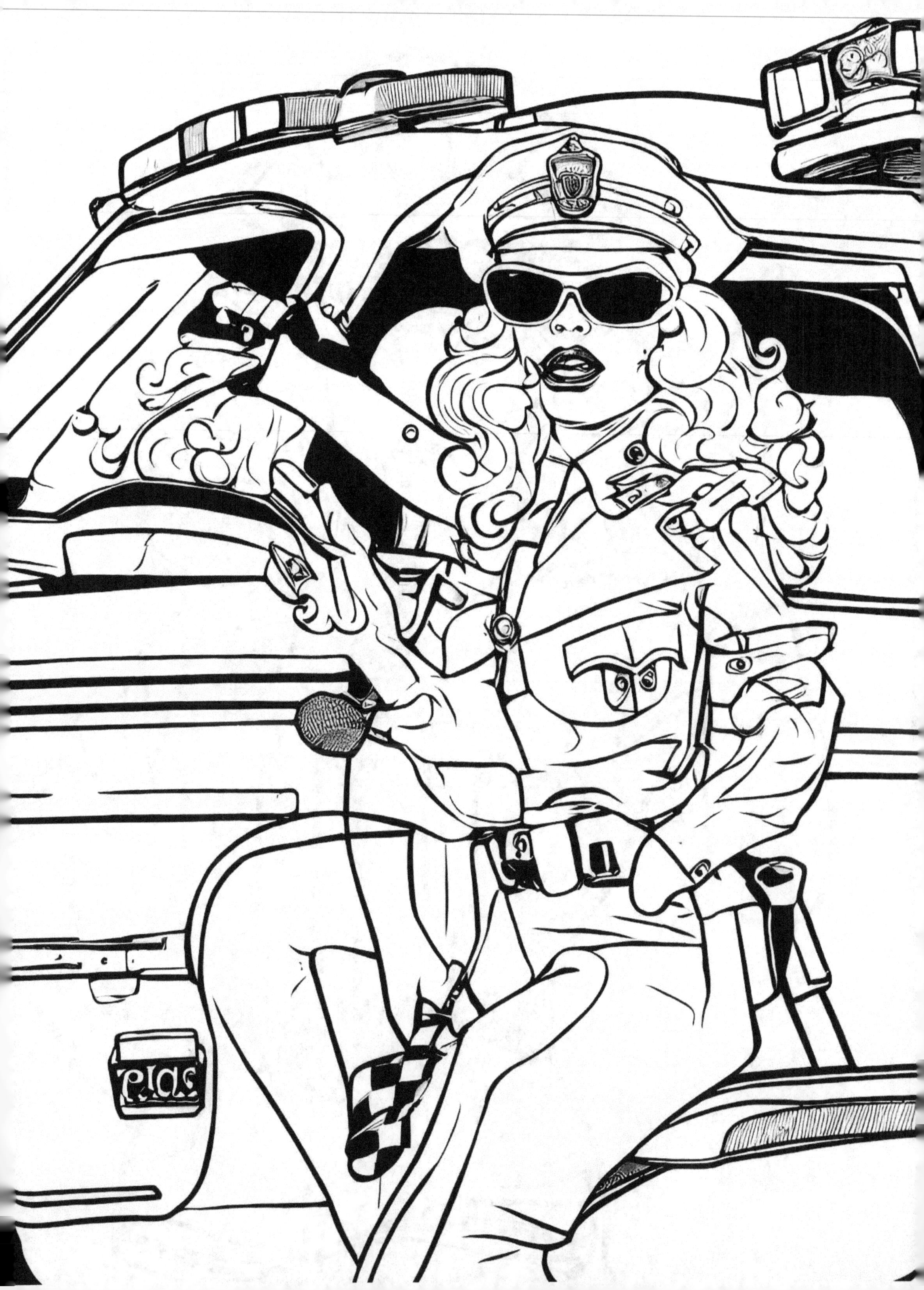

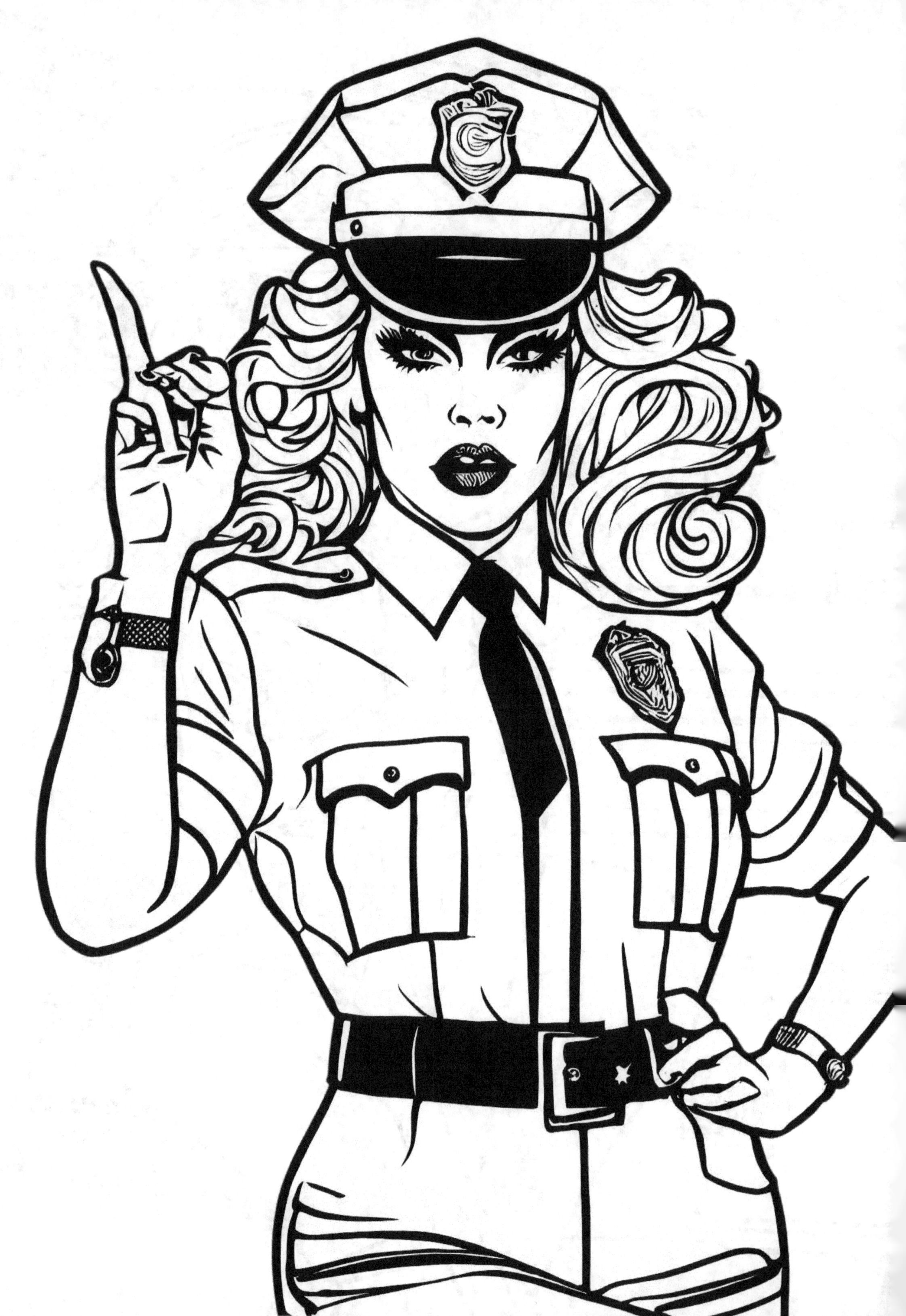

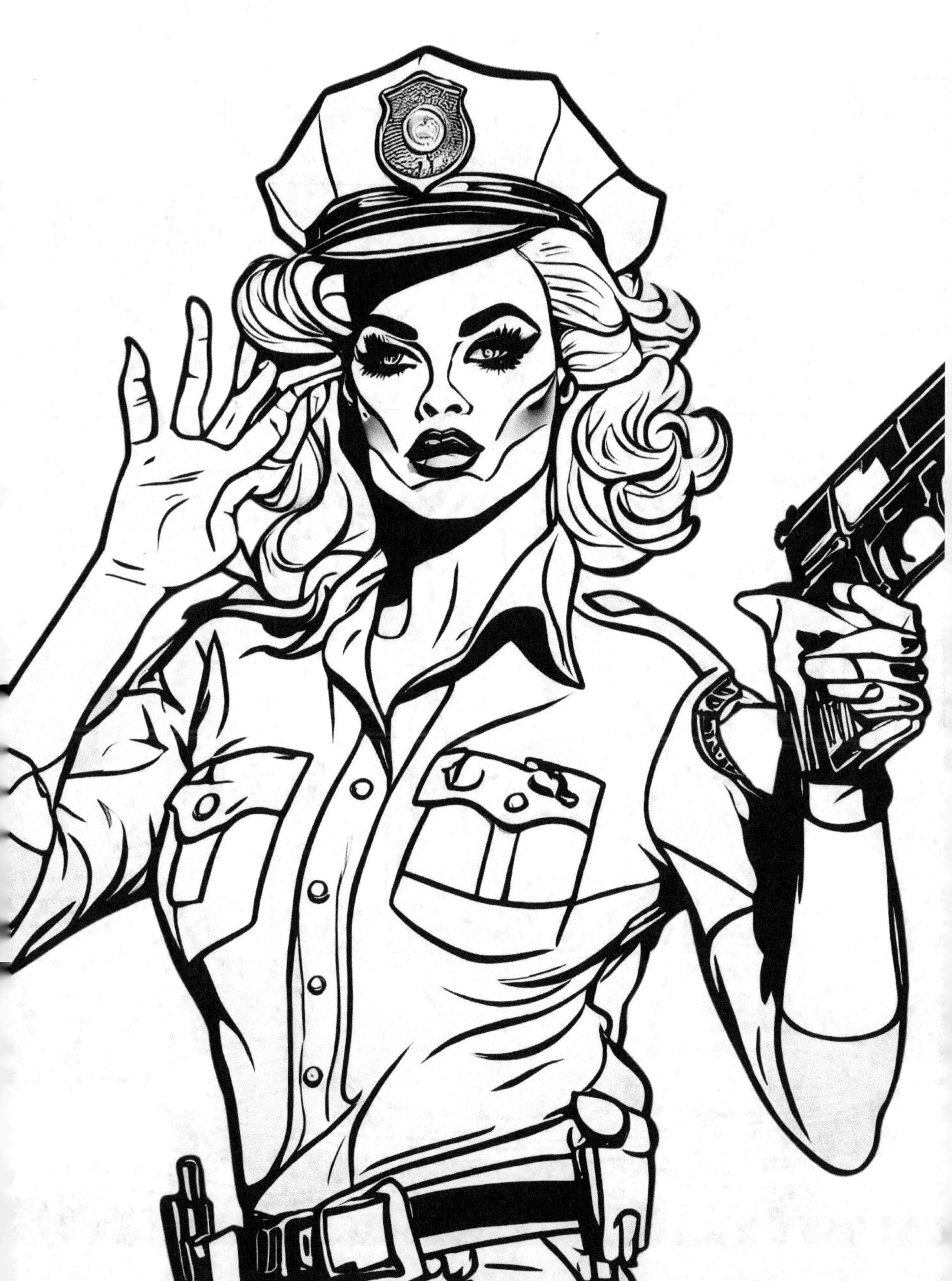

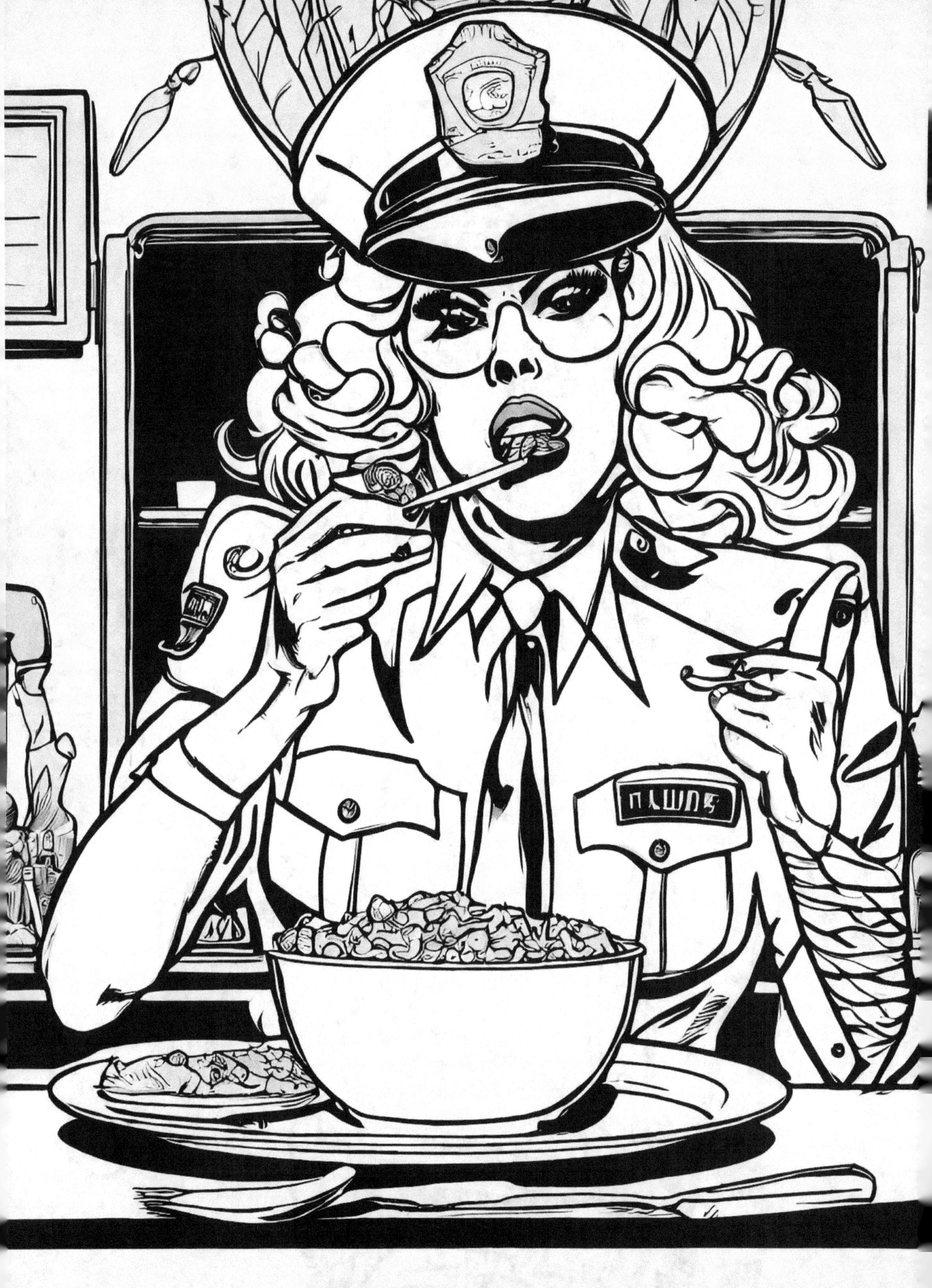

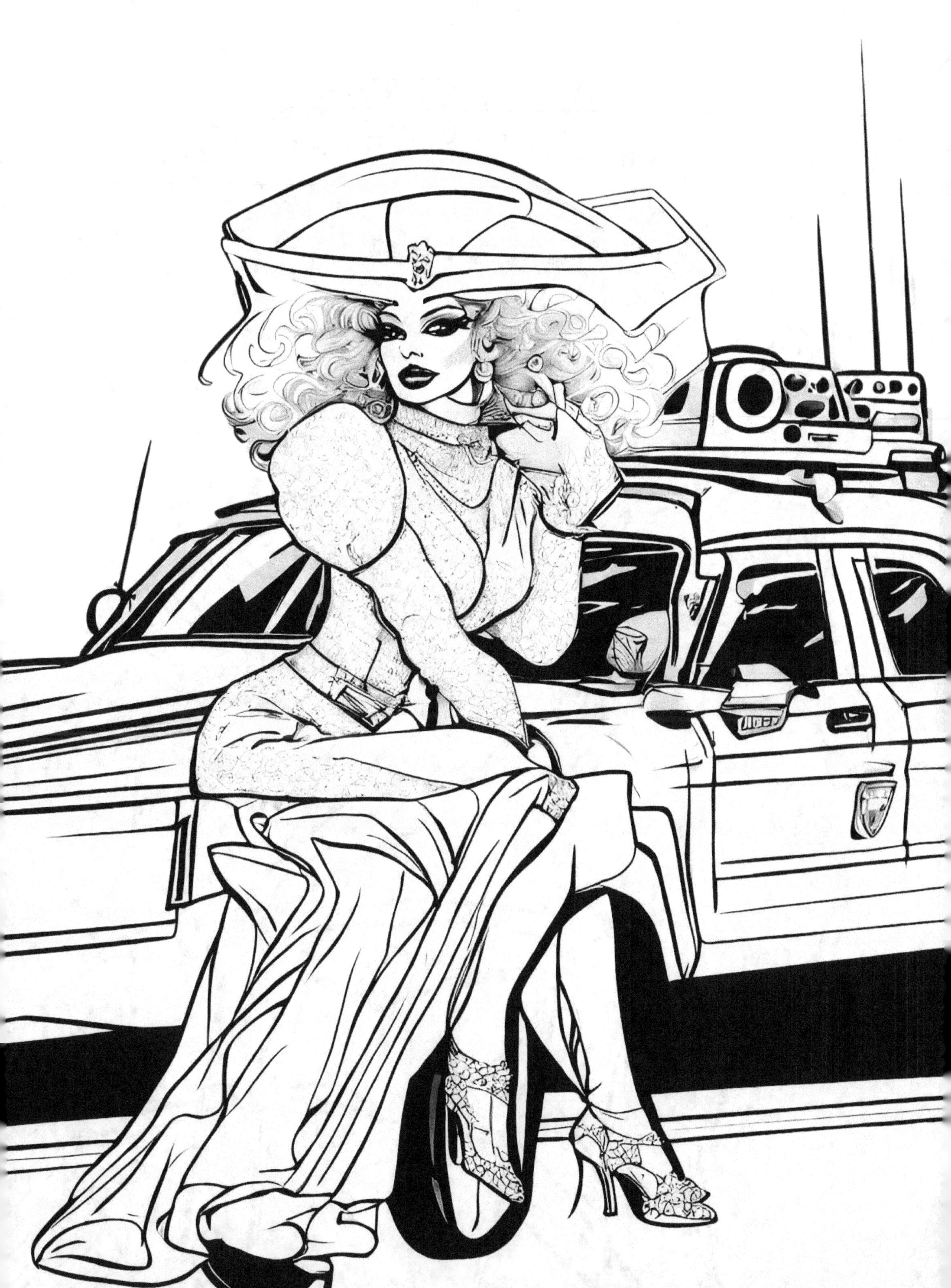

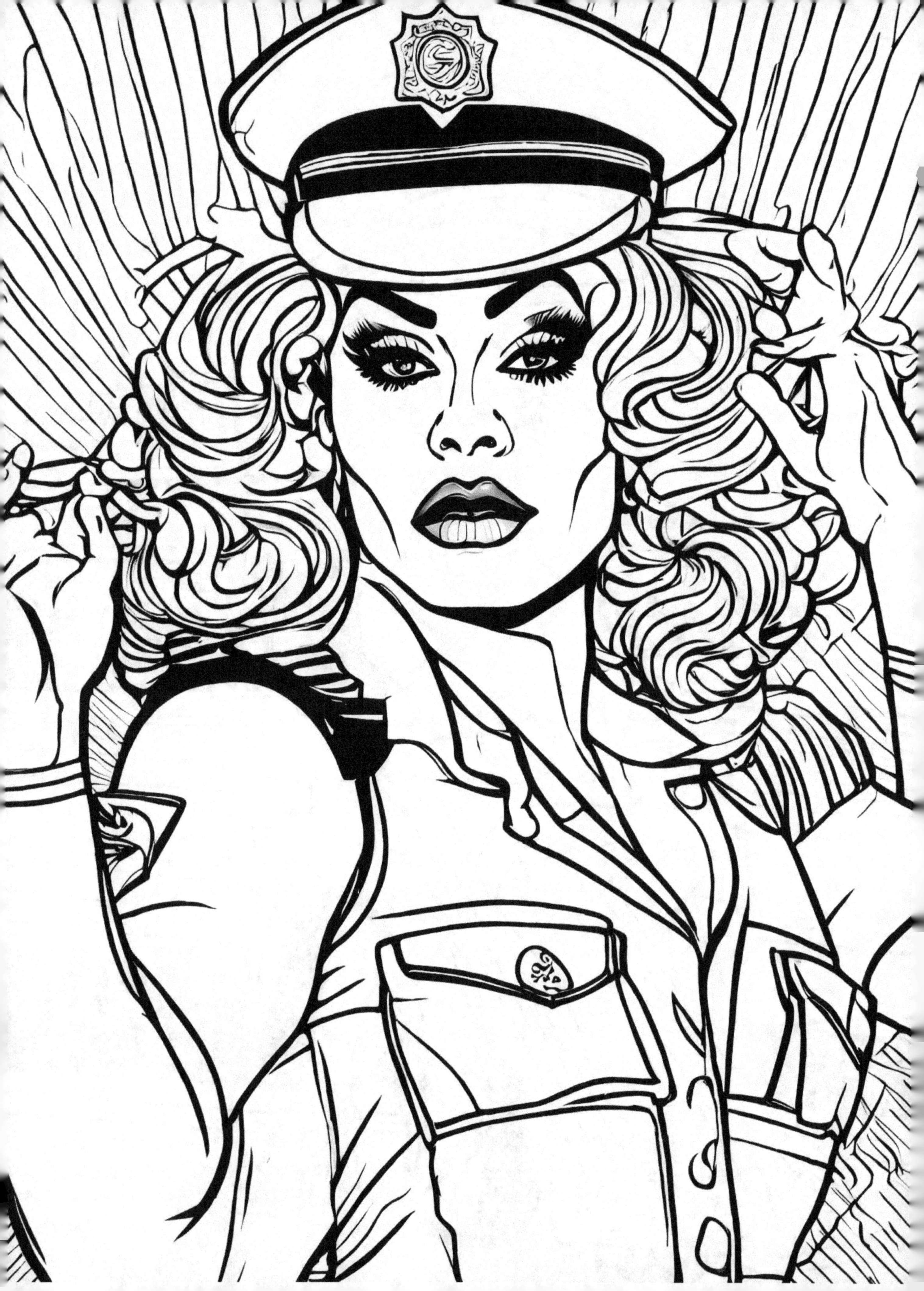

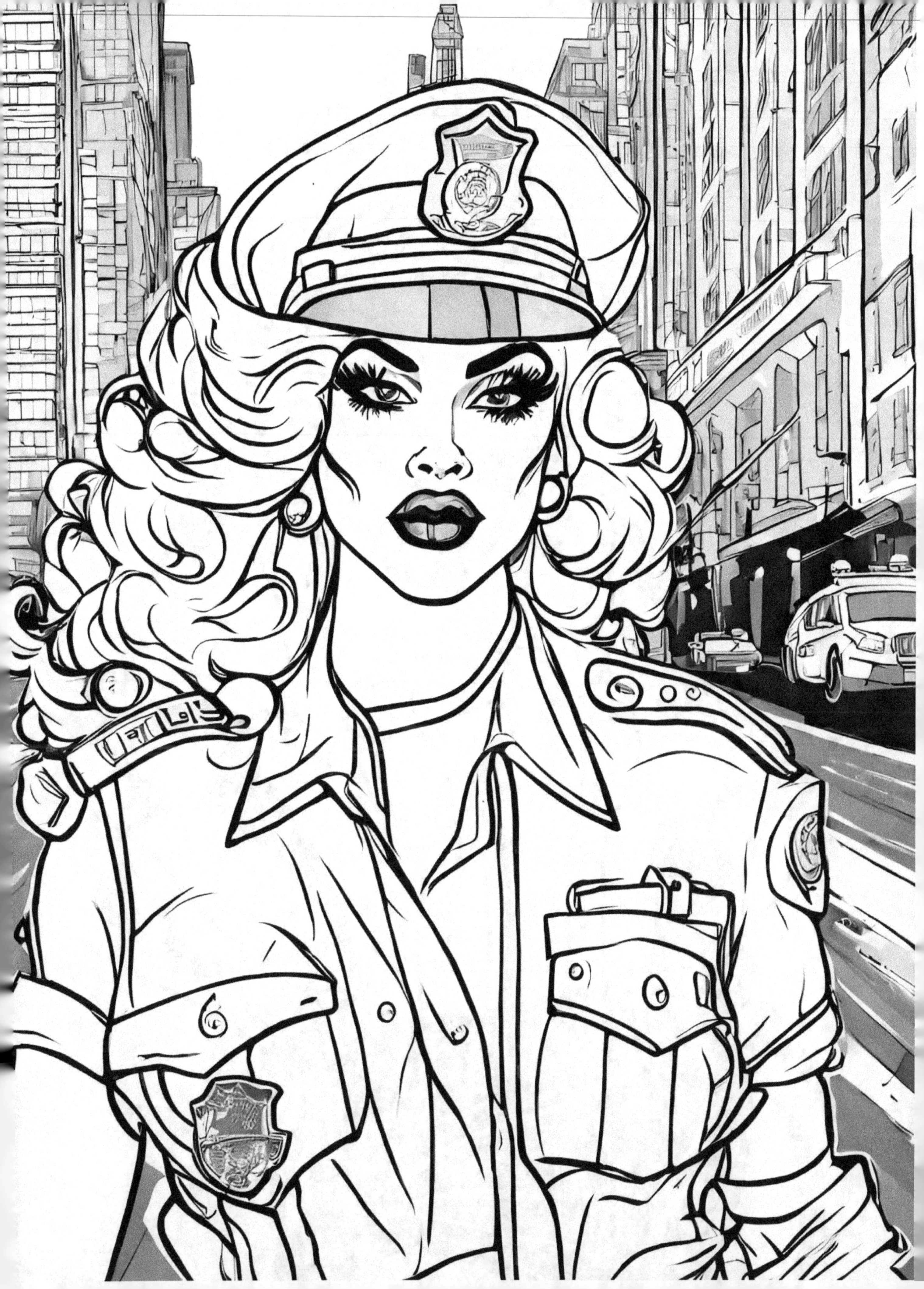

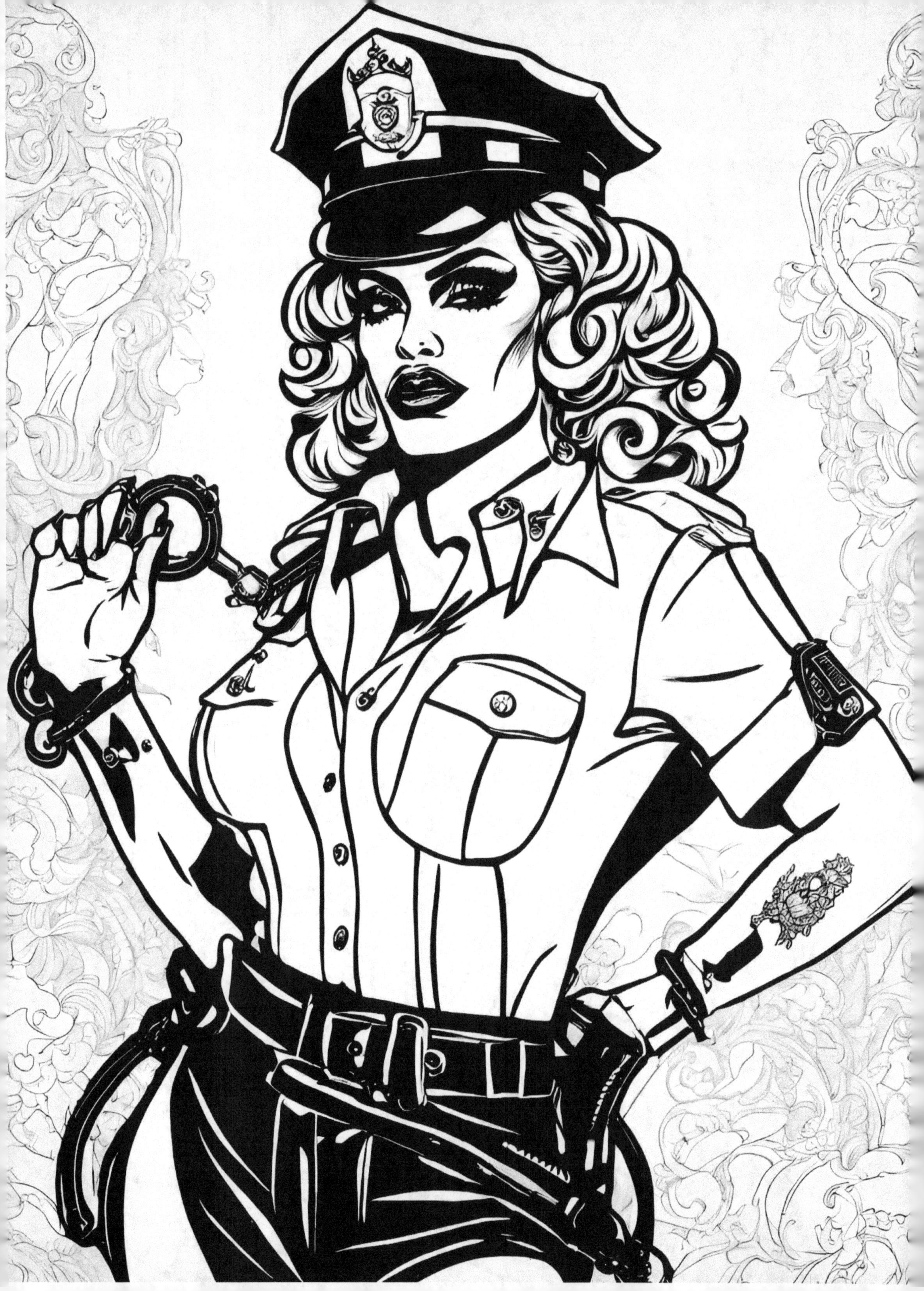

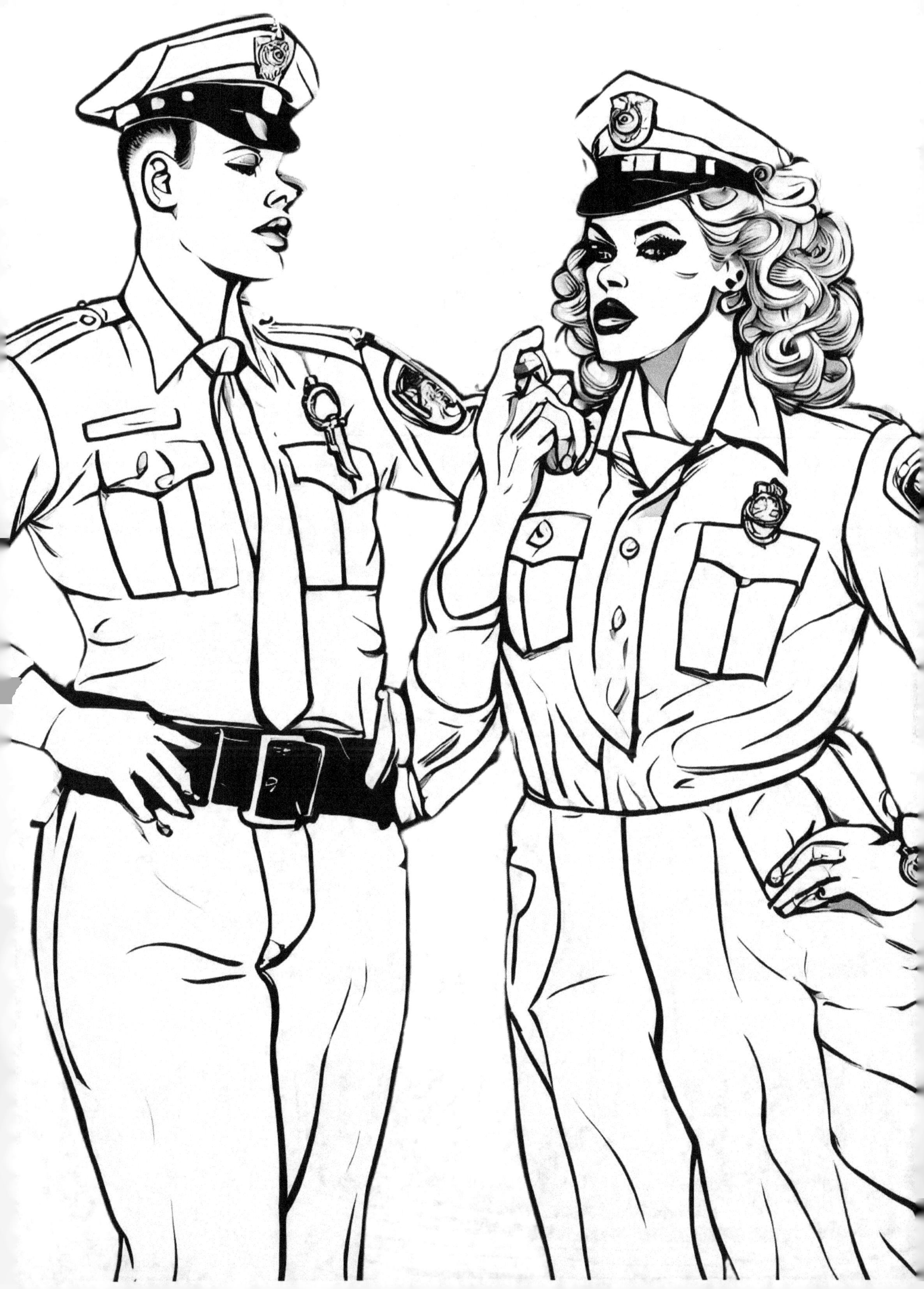

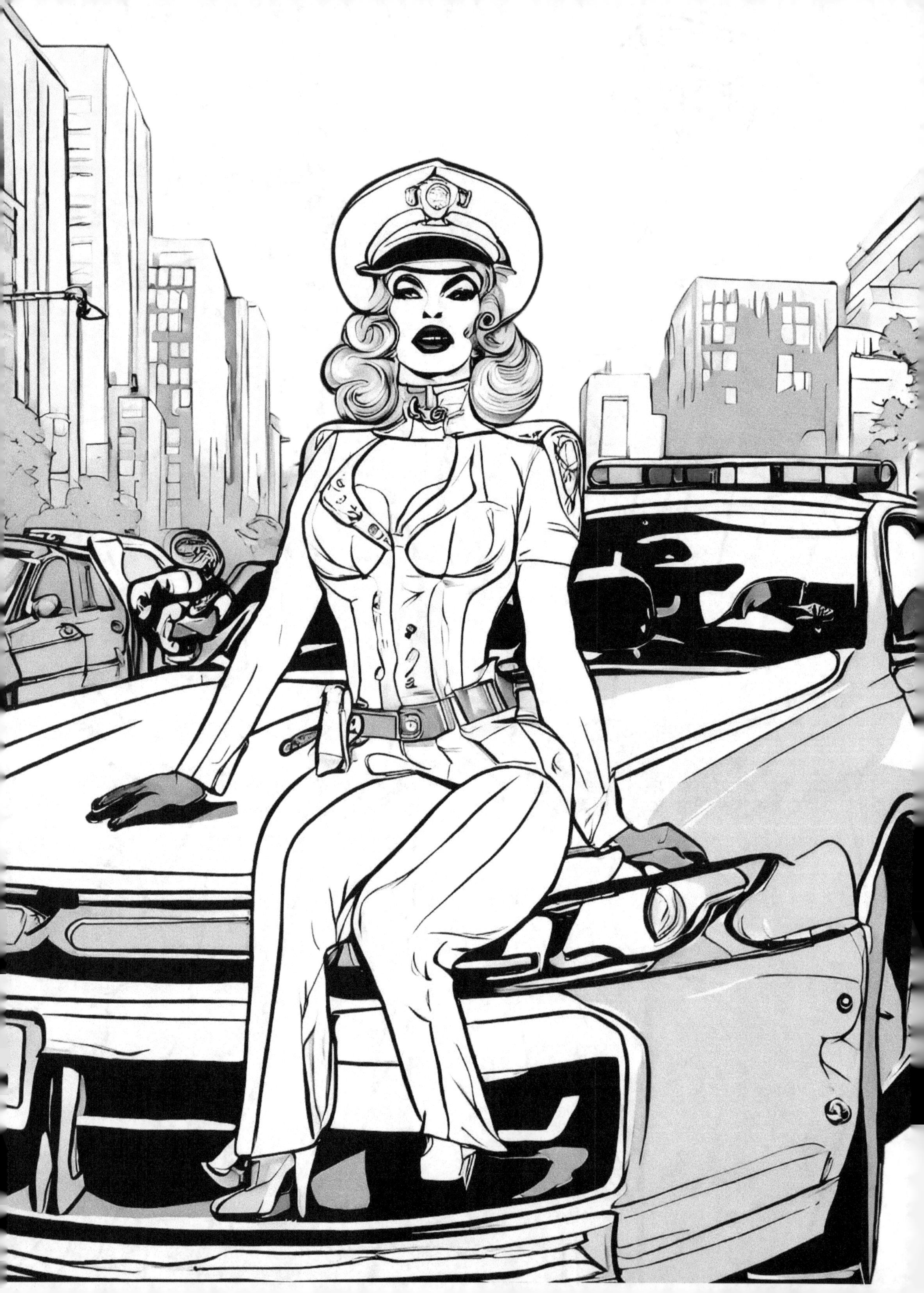

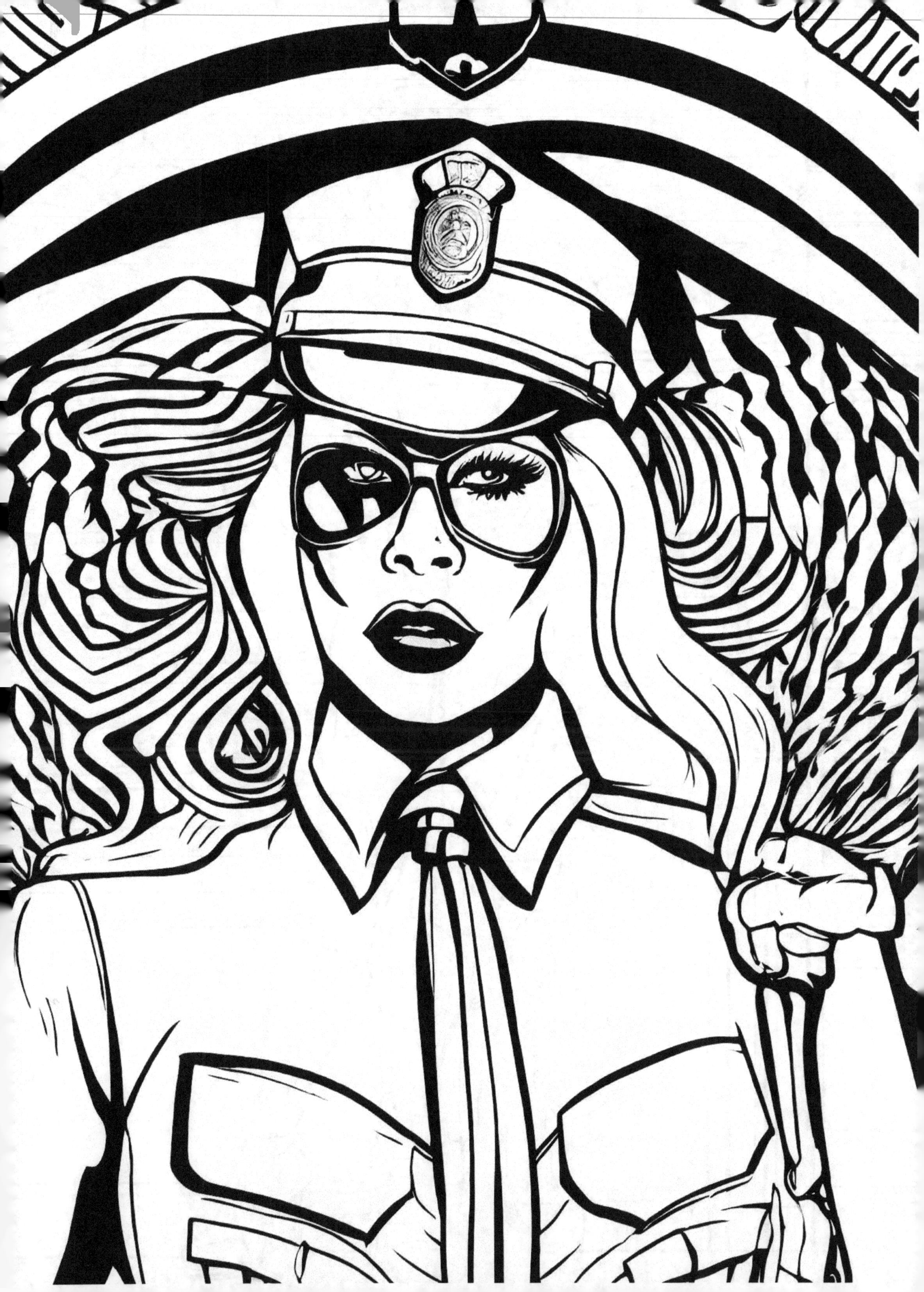

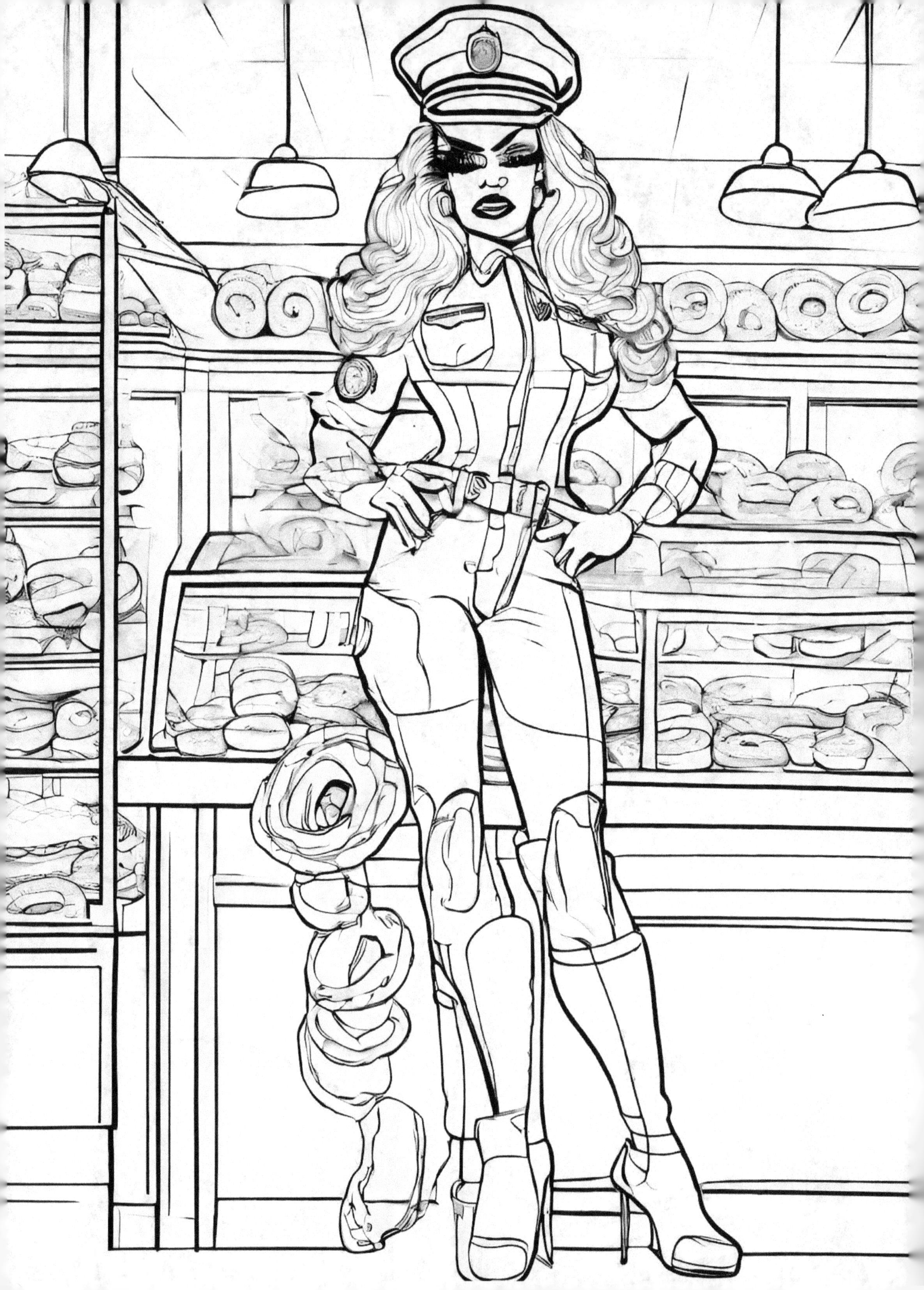

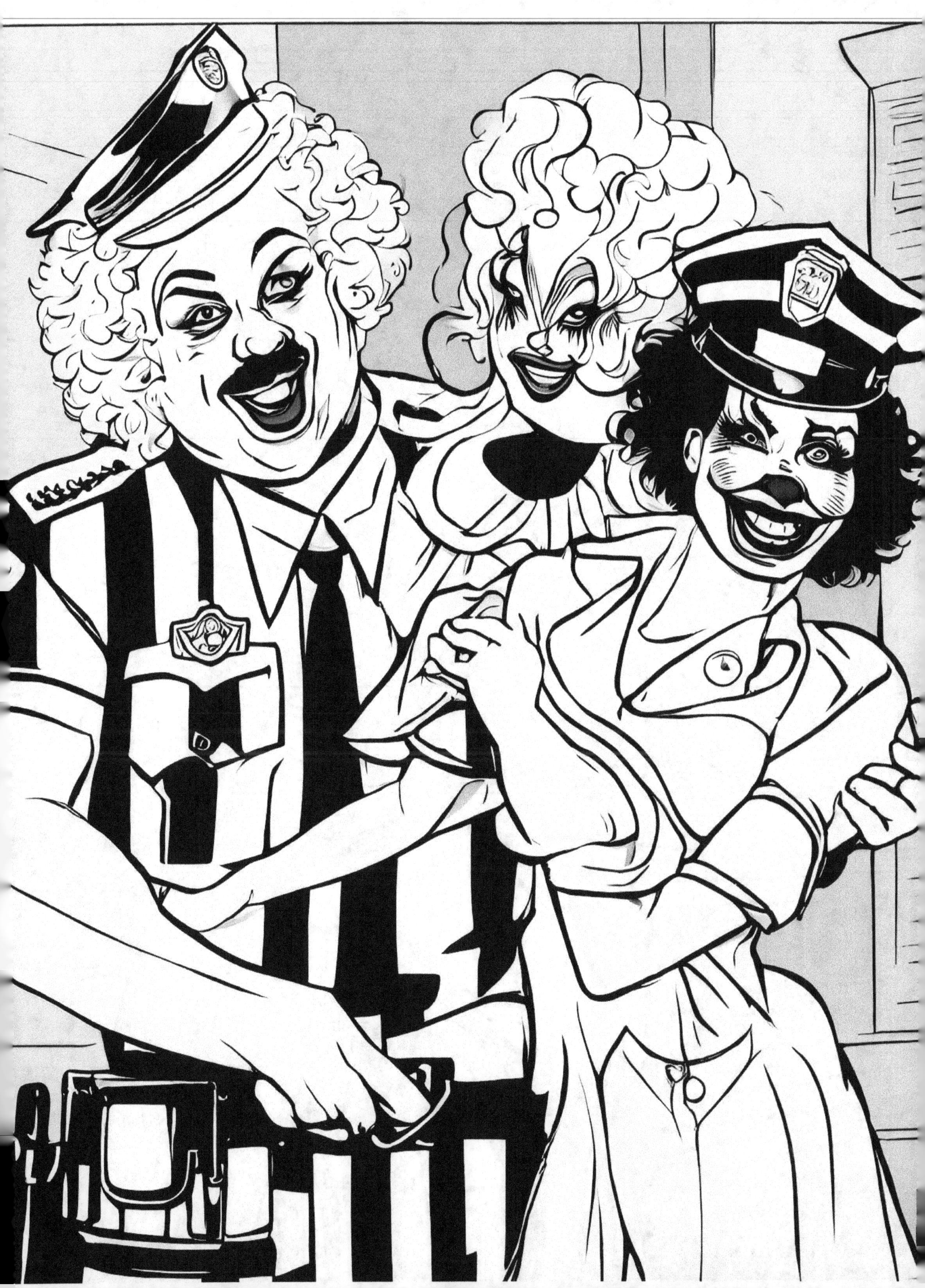

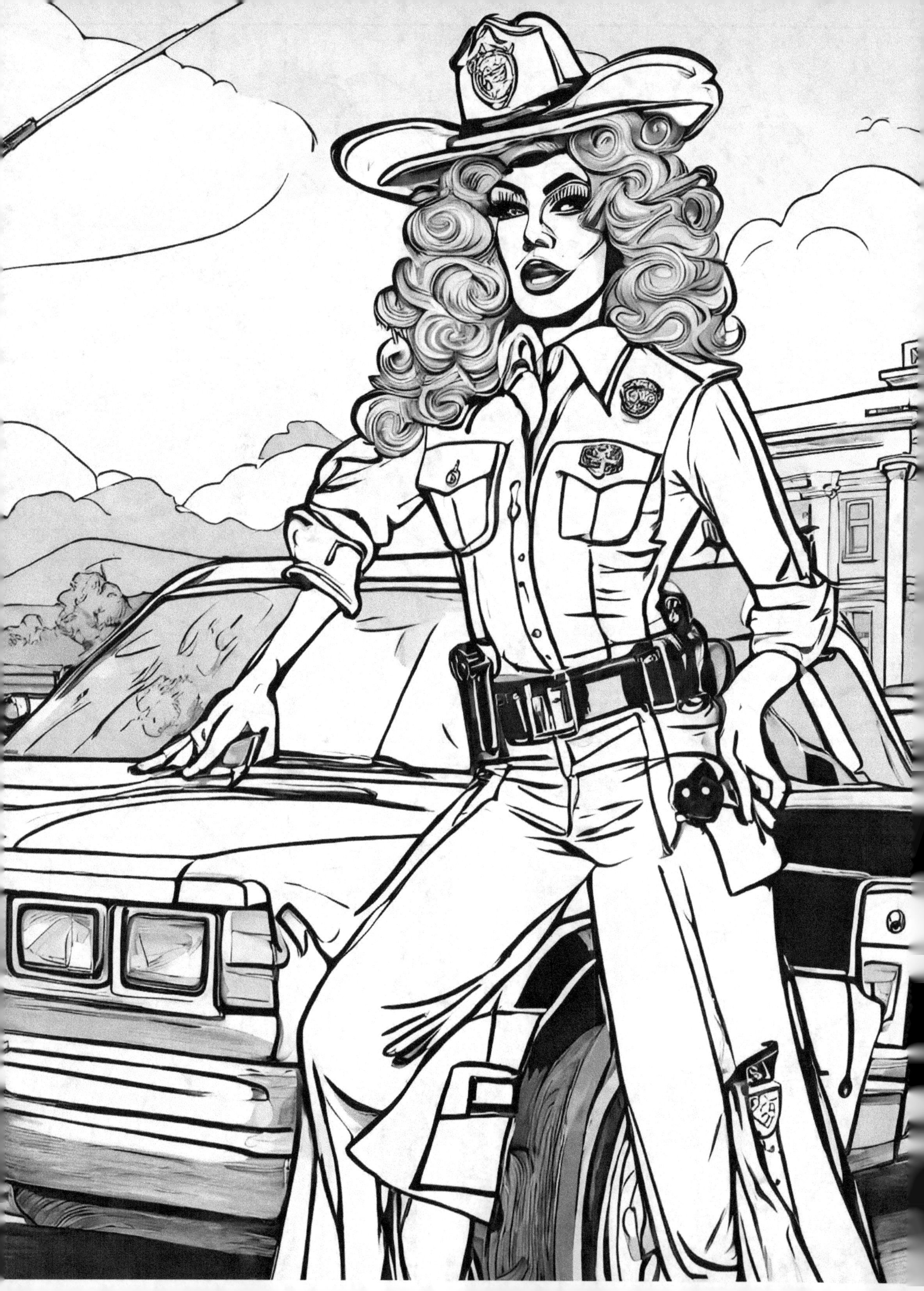

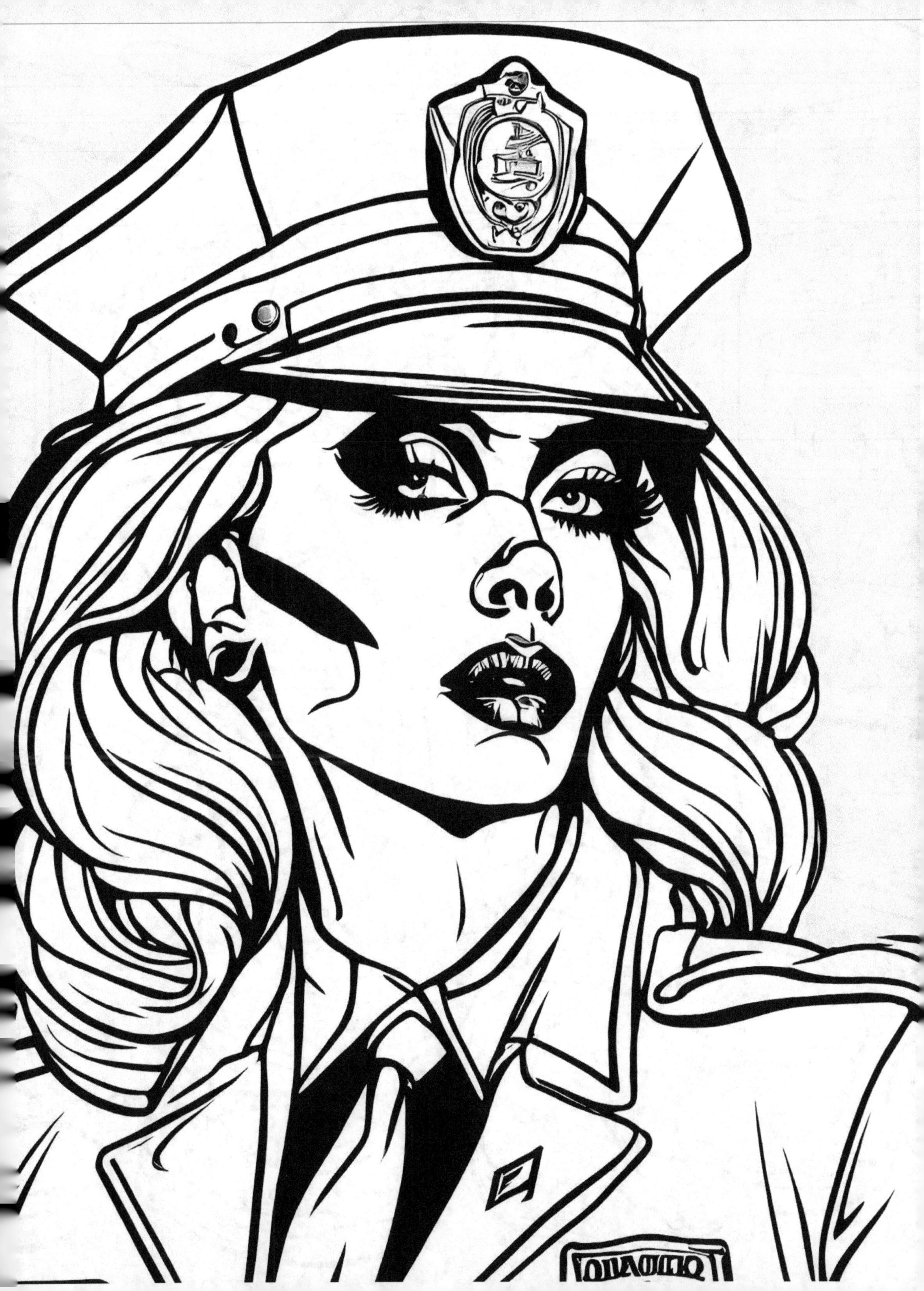

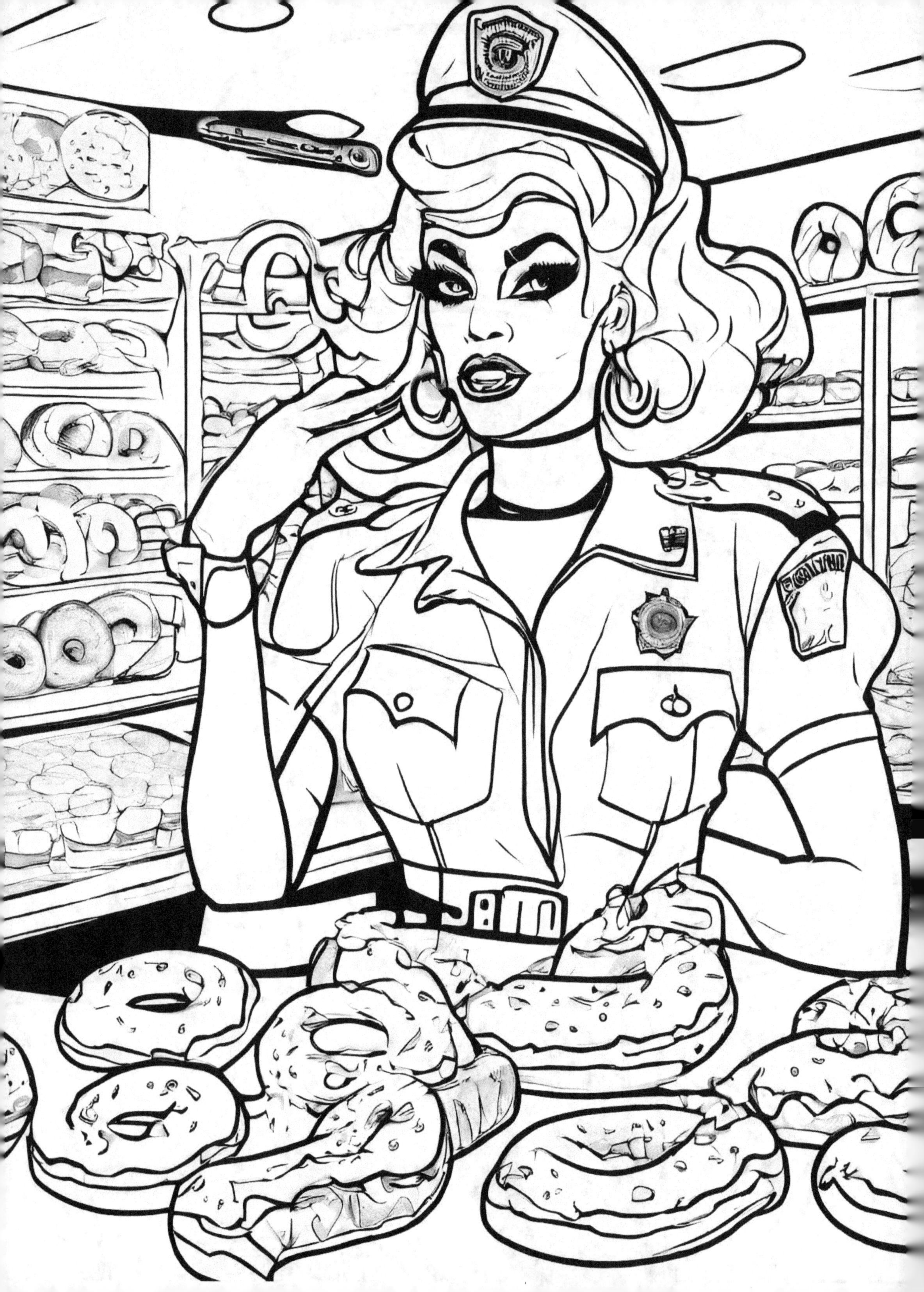

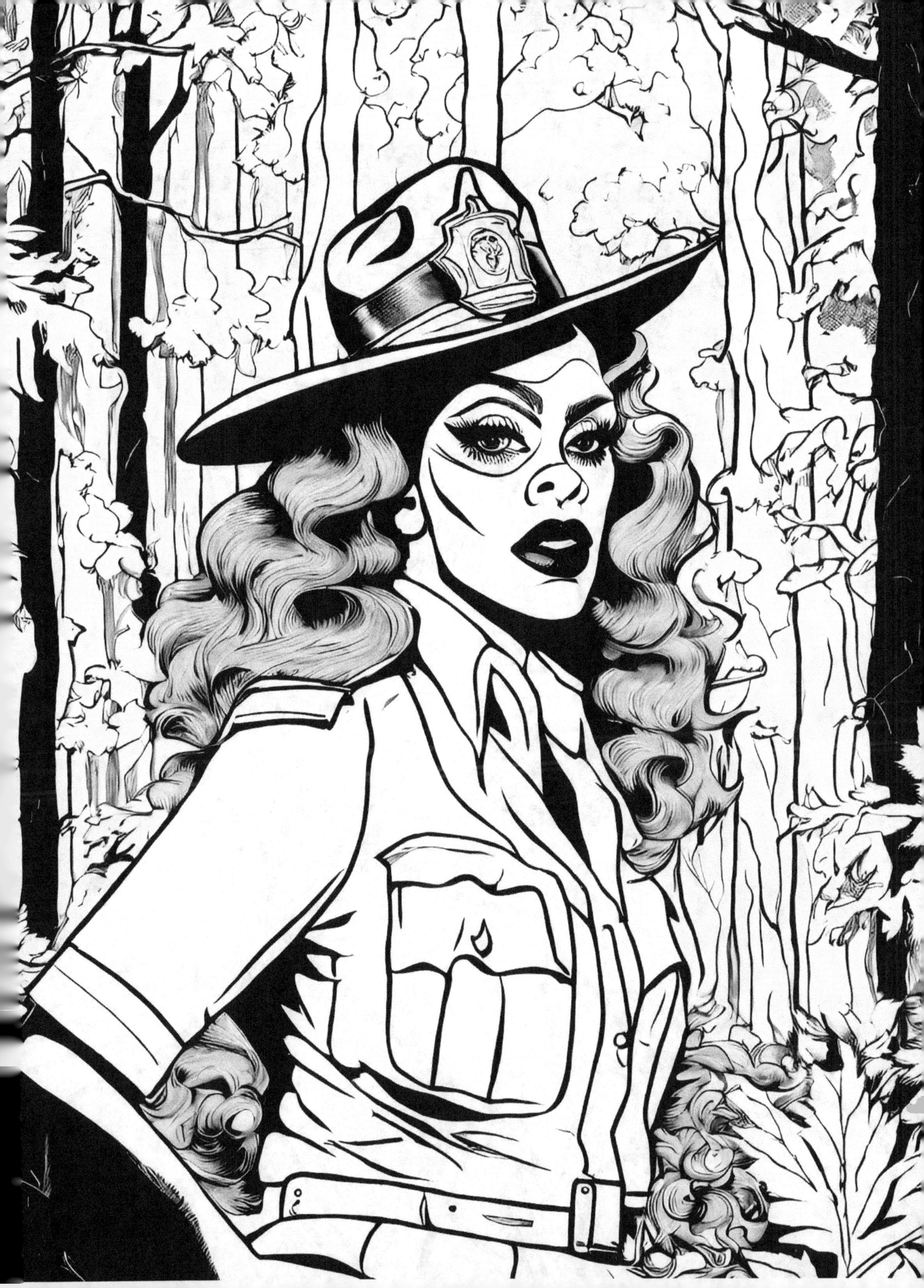

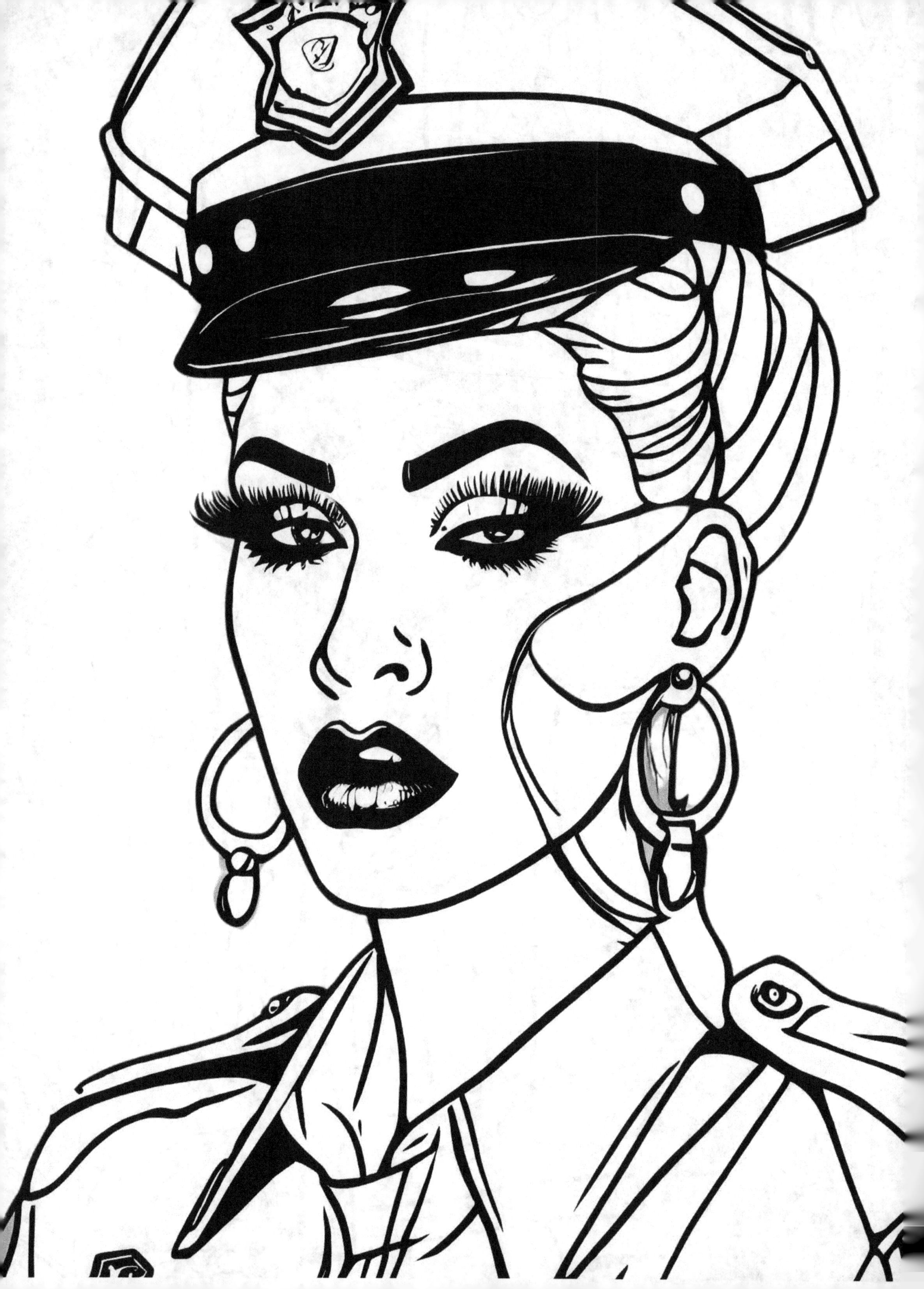

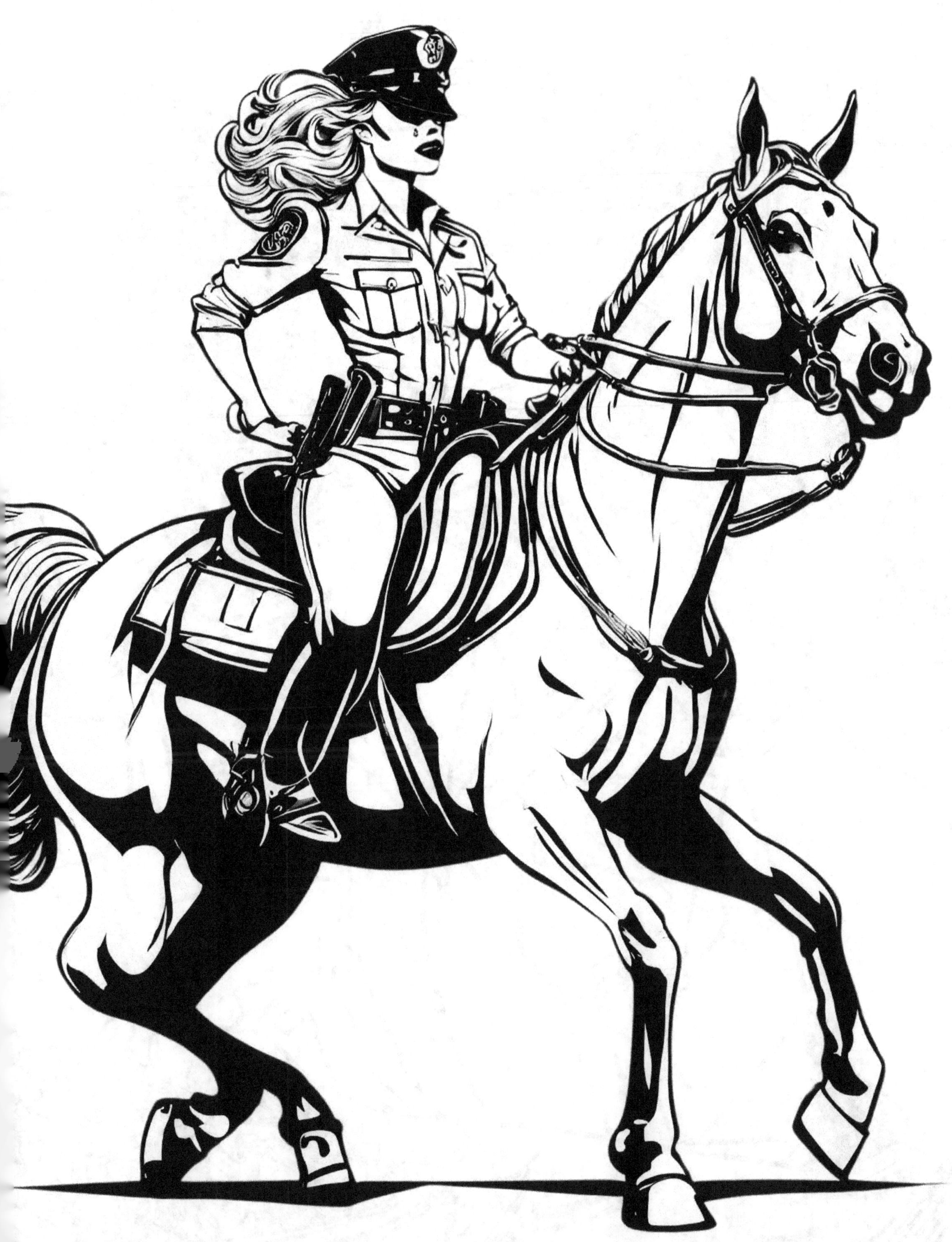

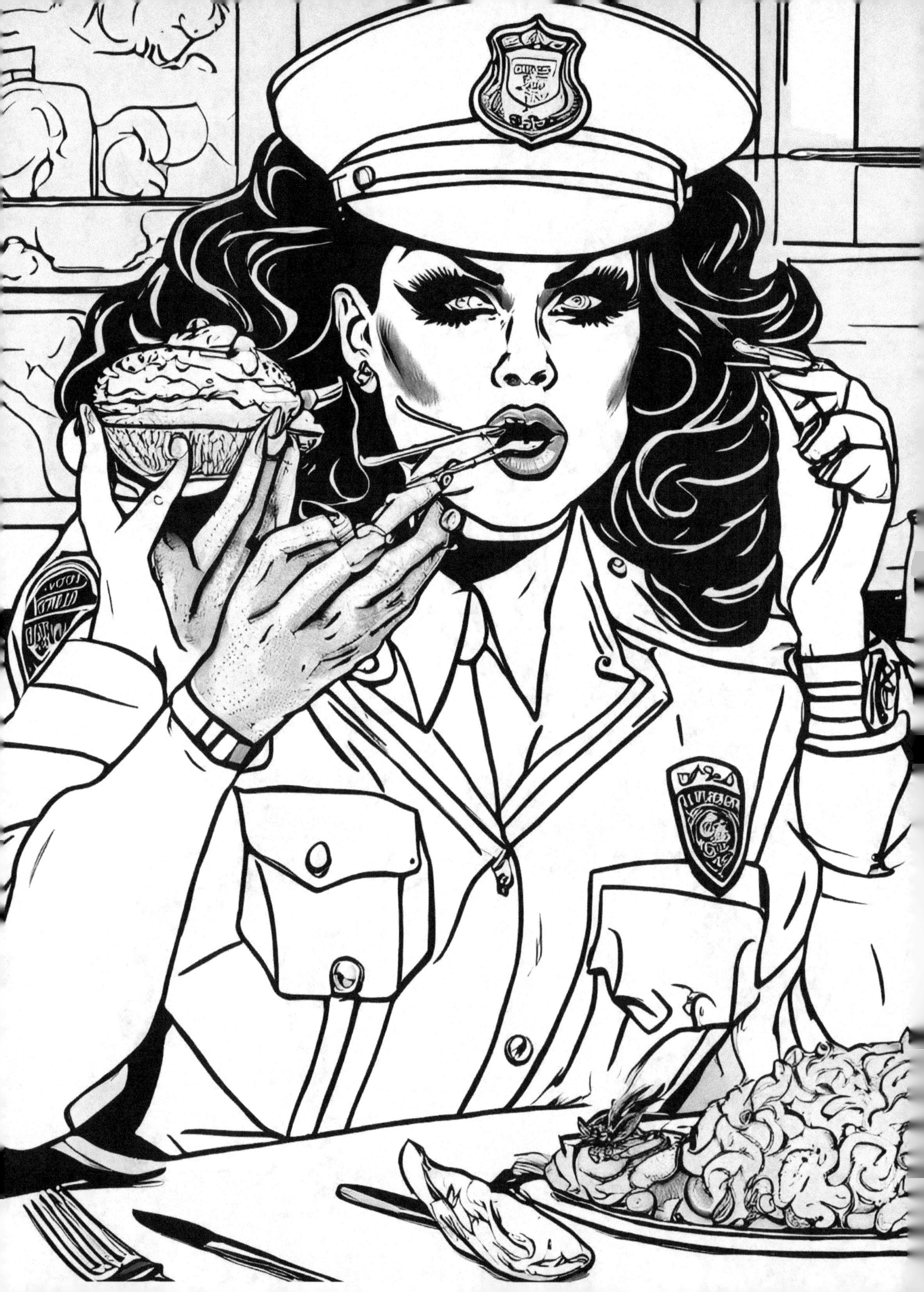

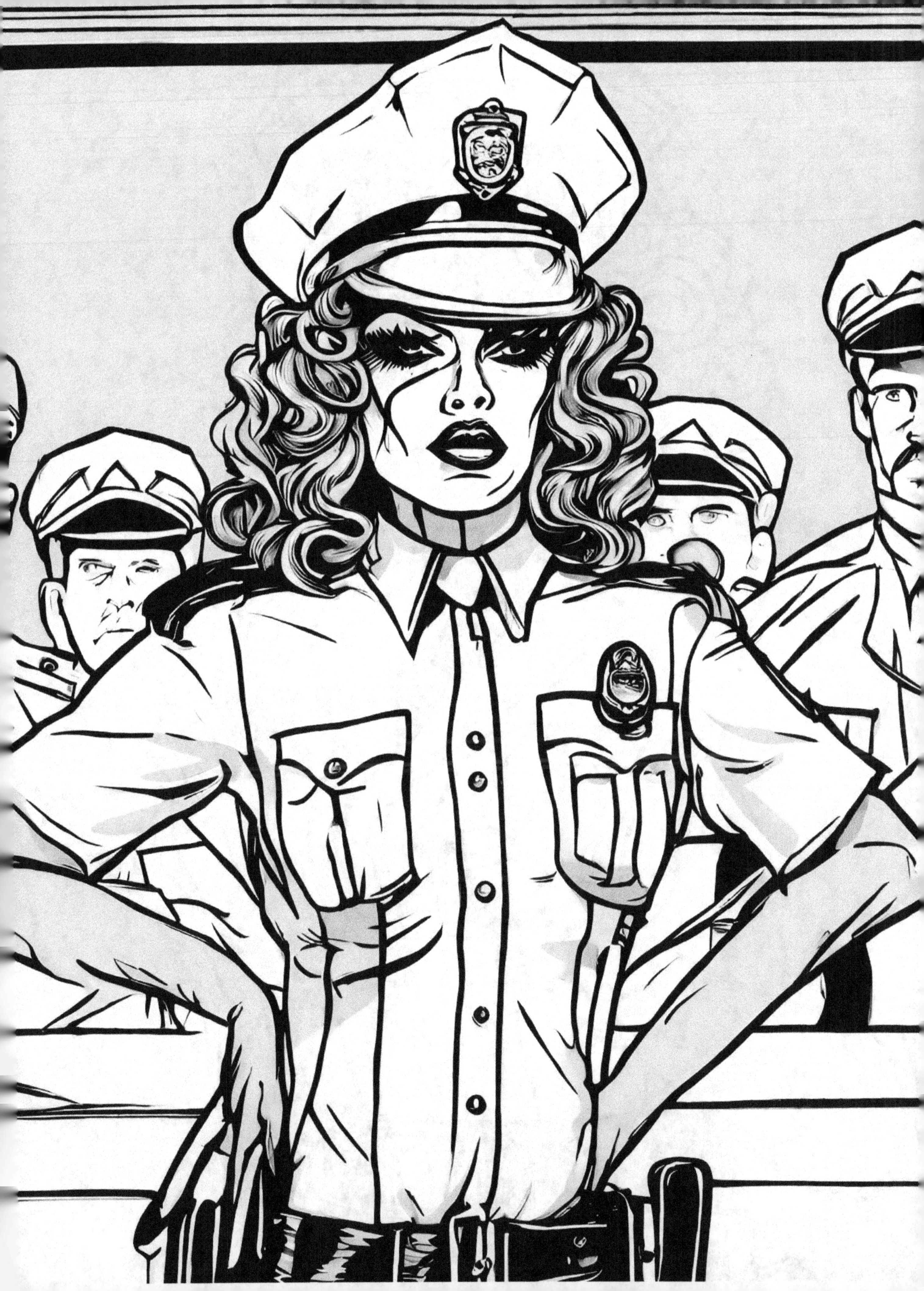

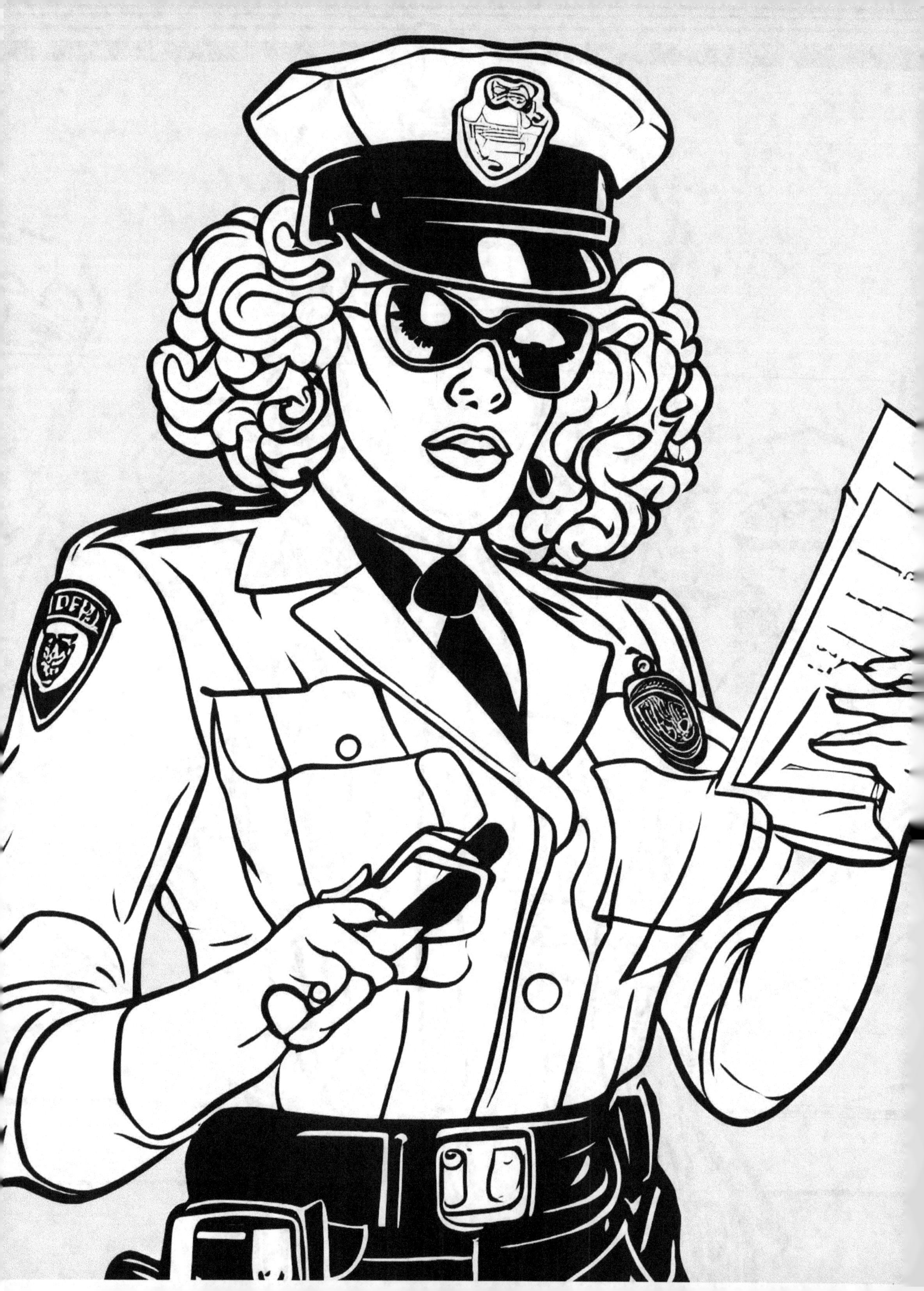